THE NORRIS, GREGG, & NORRIS

COIN

AND

THE GOLD RUSH OF '49

By
George Hull

YE GALLEON PRESS
Fairfield, Washington

Library of Congress Cataloging in Publication Data

Hull, George, 1937-
    The Norris, Gregg & Norris Coin and the Gold Rush of '49 / by
George Hull.
       p.cm.

    Includes bibliographical references.
    1. Gold coins — California — History — 19th century. 2. Coins,
American — California — History — 19th century. 3. California — Gold
discoveries. 4. Gold mines and mining — California — History — 19th
century. I. Title: Norris, Gregg, and Norris Coin and the Gold Rush of
'49. II. Title.
CJ1834.H85 2002   332.4'042'0979409034 — dc21   2002069175
ISBN 087770-741-3 (hc)
ISBN 087770-740-5 (pb)

DEDICATION

This book is dedicated with
deepest gratitude
to

JACK KLAUSEN

Who inspired me to learn more about
Territorial coins and who sold me my first one.

ACKNOWLEDGMENTS

All of the people who were of tremendous value in the completion of this book fall into three classifications.

First, for inspiration, the national titans who got me started with their assistance and challenges: Q. David Bowers, of Bowers and Merena; Donald Kagin, of Kagins; Dan Owens; and a legend in the knowledge of the history of territorial coins, Jack Klausen.

A big thanks goes to my typesetter, Lauri Naber, with her brilliant work; and the ladies that did the proofreading, Lee Pettigrew and Teresa Herlinger. The publisher Glen Adams, at age 89, was an inspiration and a source of encouragement.

Those, who without their assistance this book would never have existed, who provided expertise during the research phase of the book are listed below by states.

In Oregon:
Oregon Historical Society
University of Oregon Library

In New York:
Judith Walsh, Archivist, Brooklyn Collection; Brooklyn Public Library.
Dionne C. Harris-Jackman, Micromaterial; Brooklyn Public Library.
Joseph Ditta, Reference Librarian; new York Historical Society.
The office staff, Greenwood Cemetary; Brooklyn

In Utah:
Bruce Harmon, Bernice Blaimer, and Andrew S. Webb; Lineages.

In Colorado:
Lynn Chen, Librarian: American Numismatic Library.

District of Columbia:
Douglas A. Mudd, Collection Manager: Smithsonian Museum of American History.

Benicia, California:
Beverly Phelan, Benicia Historical Museum.
Karen Burns, Benicia Historical Museum.

Mariposa, California:
Kerry Lee Self, Curator; Mariposa Museum.

Palm Springs, California:
The staff of Palm Springs Public Library.

San Bruno, California:
Kathleen M. O'Conner, Archivist; National Archives Center.

San Francisco, California:
The staff at the California Historical Society Museum.
Tom Carey, Librarian, San Francisco Public Library.
Pat Keats, Archivist, The Society of California Pioneers.

Stockton, California:
Susan N. Benedetti, Archivist, The Haggin Museum.
Darren Williams & Serena Provencio, San Joauin County Assessors Office.
Deborah Mastel, Collections manager, San Joaquin County Historical Museum.
Alici Willis, San Joaquin County Recorders Office.
The staff at the Stockton Public Library.
Ms. Daryl Morrison, Head of Special Collections, University of Pacific Library.

TABLE OF CONTENTS

INTRODUCTION

One of the most fascinating aspects of the history of the gold rush of 1849 were the personalities of the adventurers who risked everything for the opportunity to become wealthy. Whether a dream or reality, the determinant was lady luck for a lot of the participants.

In order to capture the true flavor of the miners, the materials in this text have retained the exact quotes of the participants. Errors in capitalization, grammar, and spelling have been included in the quotes. The vernacular of the miners was as colorful as their lives.

Soon after the gold rush, the meanings of the three letters, 'N.G.& N.', on what were probably the first California territorial gold coins, were lost. Who produced the coins, and where did they go? It wasn't until 1902, fifty-three years later, that a piece of paper wrapped around one of the coins was found that said, 'from my friends Norris, Grigg, and Norris'. This paper was discovered only when Augustus Humbert's possessions were sold in 1902; he had been the U.S. Assayer in San Francisco.

Where did these three coiners go after the gold rush? It is the author's belief that this research, that provides the answers, is the first attempt to trace the two Norris brothers and Charles Gregg. This story documents most of the research in this quest.

Except for three photographs, all the pictures in the book were taken by the author. Credits for the photographs are listed below:

Picture of Hiram A. Norris' property in Stockton in 1850 - Deborah Mastel & the San Joaquin Historical Museum.
Picture of Hiram A. Norris' property in Stockton in 2001 - Caroline Photography, Stockton, California.
Picture of an 1849 Norris, Gregg, & Norris coin - Dave Simone, Eugene, Oregon.

THERE STUMBLED A MINER FRESH FROM THE CREEKS

When out of the night, which was fifty below,
and into the din and the glare,
There stumbled a miner fresh from the
creeks, dog-dirty, and loaded for bear.
He looked like a man with a foot in the grave
and scarcely the strength of a louse,
Yet he tilted a poke of dust on the bar, and
he called for drinks for the house.
There was none could place the stranger's
face, though we searched ourselves for a clue;
But we drank his health, and the last to drink was
Dangerous Dan McGrew.[1]

Robert Service, the great poet of the North, so poetically captured the lot and plight of the miner. After a long day of toil, thirst, and sweat, the miner still faced many unfulfilled needs in the primitive country of the West.

If he worked on the desert - water and salt. If he was prospecting at high elevations, the need was for warmth. Wherever, he needed rest and recuperation from a hard day of physical work.

The culture of the gold-miner was so different from the one that he had left behind in the East. An incident in Mariposa, California, in the southern gold fields, best reflects the culture. A miner and saloon-keeper had died after a drunken brawl. At the funeral, a miner proposed that the community needed to take up a collection for the distraught widow. He told the crowd, "Tiptoe Charlie, you get a gold pan

---

[1]Robert Service, Songs of a Sourdough, Ryerson Press-Toronto, 1926, Page 55.

and pass it around to each one. Start in with Rufus Lockwood. I have been told that he drinks his coffee from a cup made of ten, twenty dollar gold pieces. Anyone who can do that ought to afford a couple of twenties for this worthy cause."

Rufus, giant of a man, quickly replied, "It is a pleasure and a privilege to help a deserving and distressed woman. In the East, where I come from, no pity was extended to the distressed. I know because my own family suffered the pangs of starvation, but, thank God, out here it is different. I will start the fund with a fifty dollar Mt. Ophir gold slug and I may do even better."

Forget-the-Noise Karl replied, "You spend plenty for fire water, can't you give two or three ounces of gold dust out of your buckskin bag so that when you die, St. Peter will remember that you did some good on this earth? That's good, but just tip her a little more for good measure."

Money-to-Burn Pete replied, "I have seen you going around the country with your wheelbarrow and you always land up where there are good diggings, so why not pull out your buckskin bag and do the same as Forget-the-Noise? You know where you and your wheelbarrow can get plenty more." [2]

It was into this culture, with generosity much more common than the supply of gold coins, that the Norris, Gregg & Norris gold coins were born. The N.G. & N. coin was a story of fate, fame, wealth and Yankee ingenuity. But first a brief story of the civilization of the West.

---

[2] Newell D. Chamberlain, The Call of Gold, Valley Publishers, 1977, Page 88.

CHRONOLOGY OF THE WEST

The historical events of California were both exciting and varied. Hopefully a brief outline listing some of the more important and turbulent events will put the discovery of gold and the subsequent minting of territorial gold coins in some historical context for the reader.

Dates	Historical Event
May 1804	Lewis and Clark expedition left St. Louis
Sept. 1806	Lewis and Clark expedition returned to St. Louis
1821	Northwest Fur Company merged with Hudson's Bay
May 1827	Jedediah Smith completed the crossing of California by an American by traveling from Spring, Idaho, leaving August 7, 1826 and arriving at San Gabriel on November 28, 1826.
1833	Mexican government gave the lands back to the Indians. Mountain men were starting to see the possibilities in California and started settling its brown mountains.
1839	Johann Augustus Sutter, a Swiss emigrant, received permission from the Mexican authorities to develop 50,000 acres near the junction of the Sacramento and American rivers. He equipped his fort, in part, with gear from Russian Fort Ross.
March 1842	Gold discovered at San Francisquito, 35

1846	miles northwest of Los Angeles. General Kearny led 1600 troops followed by the five hundred volunteers of the Mormon Battalion, from Kansas to California.
July 10, 1846	U.S. flag raised at Monterey and San Francisco.
Jan. 1848	Gold discovered by James Marshall on Sutter's property on the American River near the soon-to-be established town of Coloma, California.
March or April 1849	Oregon Beaver coins minted in Oregon City, Oregon.
June 7, 1849	Gold coin by Norris, Gregg &Norris minted at Benicia; short article in the Alta California Newspaper.
July 16, 1849	Albrecht (Albert) Kuner arrived in San Francisco.
Late 1849	Miner's Bank coins minted in San Francisco.
April 3, 1850	H.A. Norris wrote the Stockton Times about the purity of the gold coins that he had minted.
April 6, 1850	400 San Francisco residents petitioned the State Legislature to establish a State Assayer.
April 20, 1850	California Legislature established State Assay Office.
July 1, 1850	State Assay Office opened at 3rd & J Streets in Sacramento.
Jan. 1851	The U.S. Assay Office opened in San Francisco, California; the State Assay Office was discontinued.
April 17, 1851	George Baldwin, coiner, shut down Baldwin & Co. and sailed to the East Coast on the Steamer Panama.

Dec. 24, 1851	Moffat & Co. Coiners, dissolved.
July 3, 1852	Congress passed a law establishing U.S. Mint in San Francisco.
March 15, 1854	First set of dies arrive at San Francisco Mint.
April 3, 1854	First deposit of gold received at the U.S. Mint in San Francisco.
April 15, 1854	First San Francisco U.S. gold coins struck.
April 4, 1860	The first trip of the Pony Express completed in Sacramento, California.
Oct. 25, 1861	Telegraph completed from New York City to Sacramento.
1862	Albert Kuner made the dies for $10 and $20 British Columbia gold coins for the Provisional Mint at New Westminister, B.C.
May 10, 1869	Central Pacific, the first transcontinental railroad, was completed at Promontory, Utah. Construction had started in Sacramento on January 8, 1963.

The first visitors from Europe were to find a primitive Eden, happily occupied by Indians who had successfully and peacefully lived in it for millenniums. "The Indians had long ago made a practical compact with nature and were effectively living off the fruits of the land. They lived at peace with the environment as well, fully utilizing their natural resources, but without plundering their stocks of game, fish, or timber. Sheltered by great natural orchards of oaks that showered down an abundance of edible acorns every fall, with a plentitude of game and fish for the taking, and natural gardens of berries and fruiting shrubs, the Indians had little need to plant crops or tend herds to support themselves. True, their search for food was sometimes an hour-by-hour preoccupation, but there was generally enough to go around."[3]

"The first Californians were distributed in a mosaic of comparatively small tribes. Although they shared common cultural patterns in shelter, clothing, hunting techniques, even mythology, they spoke more than twenty-six different languages."[4] Even with the obvious language barrier, the various tribes would swap goods with neighboring tribes; some of these products came from miles away. Obsidian was found near Mono Lake and also on the shores of Lake Paulina in central Oregon. Seashells traveled miles from the coastal tribes to the interior regions.

The concept of wealth differed from tribe to tribe. Ownership of obsidian blades was a rare status symbol. "Strings of seashells served as the universal coinage. Strung according to size on cords of standard length, they had as

---

[3]Paul C. Johnson, Pictorial History of California, Doubleday & Co., 1970, Page 29.
[4]Ibid., Page 29.

precise a monetary value as the common currencies of today."[5]
However, it didn't take long before they knew how to work the
crowd when bargaining to sell vegetables to the emigrants.
The Pima had seen enough of wagon trains to know they could
strike a good bargain. "They demanded that they be paid in
coin for their produce, or if coin was not available, double the
value in clothing."[6]

In addition to living at peace with the environment, most
tribes lived in harmony with each other. Travel, except to
tribes that lived in the vicinity, was rare. Because nature took
care of their needs, there was little purpose traveling great
distances to fight or trade for the possessions of other tribes.
The Spaniards would change all this.

The Spanish were ignorant of world geography, as was
most of Europe. They were very unaware of the unexplored
region to the north of Mexico. Being insatiable when seeking
treasure, they moved north to learn about the land that they
owned by papal right. Their leaders followed every
will-o'-the-wisp rumor of gold, gems and other precious
minerals. They formed expeditions composed of military and
church personnel; these parties penetrated the southwestern
portion of the United States.

For several hundred years the lure of gold has been a
factor in the history of California. Three hundred years before
the gold rush, Europeans dreamed of the mineral wealth
hidden in California. A widely circulated historical romance of
1510 stated, "that the island was peopled by black women
without any men among them, for they lived in the fashion of
Amazons. Their arms were of gold, and so was the harness of
wild beasts that they tamed and rode. They were ruled by
Queen Calafia, who was very large in person, the most

---

[5]Ibid., Page 30
[6]Brian McGinty, Strong Wine - The Life and Legend of Agoston
Haraszthy, Stanford University Press, 1998.

7

beautiful of them all, of blooming years, strong of limb and of great strength."[7]

"From this beguiling tale, familiar to the Spaniards who conquered Mexico in the 1520's, came the name California, first applied to the Baja Peninsula, which was thought to be an island, and then gradually extended northward to the limits of the Spanish domain in the Pacific Northwest. At the time of the conquest of Mexico in 1521, Spain and Portugal divided the world between them into two immense empires. An accommodating encyclical of the pope in 1493 allocated all new lands west of the fiftieth meridian to Spain, everything east to Portugal. Actually, neither the governments of Spain and Portugal nor the Papacy had any notion of the enormity of the territories assigned to each."[8]

When Cortes first landed in Mexico in 1519, he thought that he was walking on an island near China. The next sea explorations discovered the immense size of the Western Hemisphere. It wasn't until 1542 that Juan Rodriguez Cabrillo walked ashore thus becoming the first person from Europe to walk on what was later to become the state of California. Cabrillo was attempting to find a passage from the Atlantic to the Pacific Ocean; while doing so, he mapped the shoreline, located bays, and christened the landmarks. His ship sailed as far to the north as Rogue River, now in Oregon. In 1519, Cabrillo had led a company of cross-bowmen under Tenochitlan. His first navy command was the voyage north from the port of La Natividad, on the Pacific coast of Mexico. "His flagship, the Caravel, voyaged north, one of Cabrillo's goals was to locate the Seven Cities of Gold ruled by El Dorado, a king whose subjects dusted him with gold every morning and washed it off every night."[9]

---

[7] Paul C. Johnson, Pictorial History of California, Doubleday & Co., 1970, Page 13.
[8] Ibid., Page 13.
[9] Dale L. Walker, Bear Flag Rising - The Conquest of California

Cabrillo located a good harbor that he named San Miguel (soon called San Diego), found ways to talk to the coastal Indians, and sailed on. "He sighted but did not visit a wide-mouthed harbor 450 miles north of San Migual and named it Baia do los Pinos (probably Monterey Bay) and in mid-November, after sailing past a great fog-shrouded place that would become known in three hundred years as the Golden Gate, the San Salvador and Victoria anchored in a large bay about six hundred miles north of San Miguel. This anchorage was visited thirty-five years later by the English freebooter, Sir Francis Drake, and given his name. On the return voyage, somewhere in the islands off Santa Barbara Channel on January 3, 1543, Cabrillo died of an infection."[10]

The Spanish authorities were continually looking for a way to protect the treasure galleons as they returned to Spain from the Orient. Voyagers were ordered out onto the seas to explore the west coast to attempt to locate a shortcut back to the homeland. The master privateer, Francis Drake, landed in California in 1579 and claimed the area for England, under the name Nova Albion, to please Queen Elizabeth; this was forty years before the Pilgrims landed at Plymouth Rock. Now, colonization, military might, and safe harbors became urgent. Spanish sailors delved into the possibility of establishing a fort in Alta California, and they soon discovered two good harbors: San Diego and the open crescent at Monterey. Somehow they had all missed the beautiful harbor at San Francisco and the hidden millions of dollars in gold to the east of the harbor.

A hundred and ten years after Columbus sighted the New World, a merchant seaman, Sebastian Vizcaino sailed from Acapulco. Setting sail on May 5, 1602, he hoped to find a port along the northern coast where galleons could stop. As he sailed north, he renamed all the landmarks that Cabrillo had

---

1846, Tom Doherty Associates, 1999, Page 25.
[10]Ibid., Page 27.

previously christened. "He reserved the name of his viceroy, the Conde de Monterey, for the port he sought. On December 16, Vizcaino rounded Punta de Pinos and discovered a perfect harbor, sheltered from all winds. Though Don Gasper de Portola, governor of lower California and padre Junipero Serra would not visit the area by land for almost 168 years, the colorful history of Alta California had begun. The pre-history of the stone-age Indians rapidly gave way to the Spanish and then the Mexican colonization."[11]

Over 200 years later, in the spring of 1769, the frigate San Antonio sailed into the bay at San Diego. King Charles III had approved a colonizing effort in order to freeze out the threats of Russian control of California.

He dispatched Jose de Galvez to New Spain in 1765; Galvez originated several very successful colonizing programs in the six years that he served. "From the standpoint of the Spanish administration a threefold plan was followed in the occupation and settlement of Alta California. Religious forces resulted in the establishment of the mission, military occupation was to be secured by means of the presidio, or garrison, and civic life was to spring chiefly from the pueblo, or town."[12]

In some parts of California the natives were peace-loving so the missionaries were in charge, protected by a small group of soldiers to keep the peace. "Following - or along side - the mission compounds were the pueblos, the second stage in the grand colonial plan. Pueblos were packaged towns, planned in advance with painstaking care by the Spaniards. Pueblos were planned as agricultural centers, cow towns, occupied by experienced farmers and herdsmen, who raised

---

[11]Randall A. Reinstedr, Portraits of the Past, Monterey Savings & Loan Association, 1979.
[12]Rockwell D. Hunt, California In The Making, Caxton Printers, 1953, Page 23-25.

their crops and grazed their herd in the domains outside of town. The actual colonization of California was initiated by a two-pronged expedition dispatched from La Paz. The combined expedition of fifty soldiers, was commanded by the Governor of Baja California, Don Gaspar de Portola. Under him, responsible for spirutal matters, was Father Junipero Serra, a zealous Spaniard with thirty-five years experience in the frontiers of New Spain."[13]   "Portola took possession of San Diego July 1, 1769, established it as a presidio, and on July 16, Serra named it San Diego de Alcalia."[14]

The twenty-one missions were founded in three steps: anchor missions were located near supply ships on the coast, other missions were added one day's travel apart, and finally the third chain was located inland.

"The first structures were stockades, walled with stakes and roofed with thatch. Drafty and leaky, they were replaced with buildings formed of blocks of sun dried mud (adobes) made by the hundreds of thousands. The blocks were made by puddling soil into a thick soup, adding manure and straw as a binder, and pouring into a wooden mold. Virtually living walls, the adobes were known to sprout wild flowers after spring rains.

More durable masonry needed for flues, fireplaces, roofing, patio flooring and water pipes were kiln-fired. Pipe lengths were thrown on a potter's wheel, and roof tiles were shaped over wooden molds. Following 1790, contingents of master masons from Mexico arrived in the province and directed the building of magnificent stone churches at Carmel, Santa Barbara, San Gabriel, and San Juan Capistrano."[15]

---

[13]Paul C. Johnson, Pictorial History of California, Doubleday Co., 1970, Page 42.
[14]Dr. Platon M. Vallego, Memoirs of the Vallejos, 1914, Page 68.
[15]Paul C. Johnson, Pictorial History of California, Doubleday &

Because of the threat of Russian colonization moving south, military steps for the protection of California were urgently needed. Four forts (presidios) were built: Monterey, San Diego, Santa Barbara, and San Francisco.

After the break of Mexico from Spain in the year 1821, California was free from outside interference by a government hundreds of miles away. The power went through several shifts: from monarch to a church controlled mission system to a private ranch system where individual initiative, not religious doctrine, would enable the development of the natural resources of California. Consequently, the fortunate, those with religious, political, or military connections, became the owners of a patch-work quilt of huge landgrants. "No more than thirty grants were awarded in California by the Spaniards after 1784, but during the Mexican era, seven hundred were handed out, most of them in a rush just before the American occupation."[16]

The mission system was finally forced to turn over the mission lands and assets to private land owners. This breakup of the Catholic missions took place between 1832 and 1845. The Mexican governors split up the assets of land, livestock, tools, and other assets; these quickly wound up in the hands of friends, relatives, and those who had served them in the military. The law stated that the lands were supposed to be given back to the Indians, but this just did not happen.

The rancho was now the life of the citizens and the heart of the California economy. "Each rancho was a patriarchal enterprise, head-quartered in an adobe hacienda where several generations lived in harmony. At the start of the rancho era, most of the adobes were cold, drafty, and cheerless hovels, having no glass windows, doors, or

---

Co., 1970, Page 52.
[16]Ibid., Page 62.

fireplaces. As prosperity increased, civilized amenities were bartered from trading vessels. Some of the wealthier rancheros lived in adobe quadrangles; the houses, built around a patio, had their form copied a century later by Westerners seeking a gracious architectural style for large dwellings."[17]

The famous historian, H.H. Bancroft wrote, "The Californians were kind-hearted and liberal; a person could travel from San Diego to Sonoma without a coin in his pocket, and never want for a roof to cover him, a bed to sleep on, food to eat, and even tobacco to smoke."

With the collapse of the mission system, the table was being set step-by-step for the gold rush. Great land holdings, which would later provide a lot of the ground for the prospectors and miners, were formed by the authorities in Mexico. "Following the break-up of the missions, the Mexican government lavishly gave away the province to private landholders who could satisfy the governor that they could successfully raise cattle.

Under the law, the minimum grant was about six and a half square miles, the maximum eleven times this area, but property owners could acquire additional acreage by purchase or trade without official interference. "Acreage of this magnitude was needed to provide adequate pasturage for the three hundred thousand animals released from mission care into private hands. Most of the ranchos in operation by the time of the American takeover were modest affairs, handled by the men in the family with only a few Indian vaqueros."[18]

One of the great land holders in the northern part of the state was Mariano G. Vallejo who controlled over a hundred square miles of ranch land north of San Francisco Bay; it had been granted to him in 1834. He was also the military

---

[17]Ibid., Page 62.
[18]Ibid., Page 64.

13

commander of the region which separated the Russians at Ft. Ross, to the north, and the Mexicans to the south. Vallejo started the town of Sonoma where he built a large home, and where he gave work to two thousand Indian laborers.

Another patriarch of mission lands was a Swiss immigrant, John A. Sutter, who would figure prominently in the gold rush. His property, named New Helvetia, was the trading center and place of employment for several hundred Indians. He not only raised crops, had cattle, and built a fort, but he controlled the routes to the mountain passes to the east. His fort, on the Sacramento River, was the gateway to untold riches waiting to be discovered; the stage was set for the greatest gold rush in the history of the world.

About that time Jedediah Smith was entering the state of California, being the first mountain man to do so. He had left Salt Lake in 1826 and upon entering the state had been rudely received and treated with suspicion.

Trappers also entered the state from Taos and Santa Fe; they had trapped the rivers and streams of Arizona, New Mexico and Utah, but in 1829 Ewing Young led a trapping expedition west from Taos. After several months, part of the party returned to New Mexico, but Young and his faithful continued west until they crossed the Mojave River, crossed Cajon Pass, which led to San Gabriel. From there they went to San Fernando and into the San Joaquin Valley by climbing over Tejon Pass. They spent the spring of 1830 trapping beaver with a party of Hudson's Bay trappers, led by Peter Skeene Ogden.

The next fur trapper of consequence was Joseph Reddeford Walker, who blazed another route into California down the Humboldt Valley and on to Mission San Juan Bautista, where he left most of his men. He went to Monterey and got permission to stay in California. Half a dozen of his men preferred to stay in California, including George Nidever, of subsequent fame as a grizzly-bear hunter, a crack shot, and

a long-time resident of Sant Barbara. With the remaining
fifty-two in his group, Walker started up the San Joaquin Valley
in the spring of 1834. Crossing the Sierra by the wide and
easy pass that has carried his name ever since, he came out
upon Owens Valley. Of Walker's numerous discoveries on this
expedition, including the Yosemite, the Sequoias, Walker pass,
and Owens Valley, the greatest historical significance attaches
to the route to California, which he had pioneered by way of
the Humboldt Valley and a central Sierra crossing. "With
certain modifications, this trail was to prove the most popular
for the pioneer settlers, the forty-niners, and the first railroad
builders."[19] The pathways had been opened; the gold-rush
was not far behind.

In the eastern portions of the United States, California
had acquired a reputation as a land of milk, honey, and
tremendous riches. Yes, the land did belong to the sovereign
republic of Mexico, which did a weak job of governing it, but it
was still of interest to the American government. As the
sailors, trappers, and explorers brought back glowing reports of
the area, talk increased about adding the area to the United
States.

Thomas Jefferson Farnham called upon the American
people to grab the neglected prize. In the 1830's his writings
told the people in the east, "It may be confidently asserted that
no country in the world possesses so fine a climate coupled
with so productive a soil. But its miserable people live
unconscious of these things."[20]

The government was completely aware of the value of
the Pacific Coast, and started negotiations for its purchase
from Mexico; it was President Andrew Jackson who started

---

[19]John Walton Caughey, California, Prentice-Hall, Inc., 1940,
1953, Page 198.
[20]Paul C. Johnson, Pictorial History of California, Doubleday &
Co., 1970, Page 77.

these talks. The President sent a representative to Mexico and offered a purchase price of $500,000. The talks went on for six years, but the purchase was never concluded. Proposals included buying California with Oregon, California with Texas, and an offer to buy San Francisco Bay.

James K. Polk pledged in 1845 to take California by any means; he made this promise when he entered office. "Thomas O. Larkin, United States Consul in Monterey, with full authority from the President, recruited leading Californians to the cause of independence and pledged American protection for the proposed colony."[21] However, Americans, fed up with the current situation, took matters into their own hands and declared an independent republic in 1846. At the same time British emissaries in Mexico City were trying to buy California for England. The British were very optimistic about acquiring the area from Mexico because the Mexican Republic was indebted twenty-six million dollars to British financial interests. The British proposed that they would trade the debt for the area of California; by so doing the defaulted bonds would be liquidated. But while the British warships awaited orders, trouble broke out on June 14, 1846, when a group of ruffians proclaimed an independent nation, popularly known as the Bear Flag Republic. The Republic only lasted 25 days during the summer.

"Because of excessive tariff duties and increasing economic problems, most of the people were miserably poor."[22] "About the first day of April, 1846, General Jose Castro, naturally humane and generous, caused to be issued and posted up at Sonoma and various other places - the temporary residences of the newly arrived emigrants - a proclamation, ordering 'All foreigners, whose residence in the

---

[21]Ibid., Page 78.
[22]Simeon Ide, The Conquest of California by the Bear Flag Party, Rio Grande Press, Inc. (A copy of Ide's diary written in the 1840's and 1850's), Page 107.

country was less than one year, to leave the country, and their property and beasts of burden, without taking arms,' on pain of death."[23]

The next step was the seizure, early in June, by Ezekial Merritt and a dozen other Americans of a large band of government horses which General Castro had obtained from General M.G. Vallejo at Sonoma and which were being driven to San Jose by way of Sutter's Fort. This was an act of war, and it was decided that the third step must be the capture of Sonoma, the chief stronghold of the Californians north of the Bay region. The actual capture of the quiet little pueblo at early dawn, June 14, 1846, was a ludicrous affair.

Captain Fremont, later a candidate for the presidency of the United States, was mysteriously in the Sacramento Valley. Twice, after being treated very favorably by the Mexican authorities for several months, the Captain was ordered to leave California by General Castro. After leaving northern California and traveling to the area of Klamath Falls, now in the state of Oregon, Fremont was overtaken by Lt. Arthur Gillespie who delivered a secret message. The contents of the message will probably never be known, but immediately Fremont and his gang of explorers turned back south to the Sacramento Valley.

Dr. Platon M.G. Vallejo, a small boy at the time of the rebellion, remembered the incidents as fun and a lark. In the early morning of June 18, 1846, a ragged band of men surrounded the Vallejo home and, 'a huge Kentuckian, Dr. Robert Semple, found a voice and told General Vallejo that they were acting under orders from Captain Fremont to seize and hold the village of Sonoma. General Vallejo agreed to surrender and a treaty was drawn up. The group then arrested Vallejo, Jacob P. Leese, a well-known American who had built the first frame house in San Francisco, and Victor Prudon, a French gentleman, and took them to Fremont. Without regard

---

[23]Ibid., Page 109.

to morality, the surrender document, or the laws of the time, they imprisoned them for two months. The destruction and mistreatment of innocent people like the American treatment of the Indian nations, continued. They were held, "in a small room, entirely devoid of furniture or bedding, with no provision for cleanliness or sanitation, served with the coarsest and most unwholesome food, without the right of communication."[24] All of this without being charged for any violation or crime.

Then followed the erection of the Republic of California under the leadership of William B. Ide. To signalize it, William Todd designed a flag from a piece of unbleached cloth five feet long and three feet wide. It was ornamented with the red flannel of a shirt from the back of one of the men, and christened by the words 'California Republic, in red paint letters on both sides. "The mechanism of the flag was performed by Wm. Todd of Illinois. The grizzly bear was chosen as an emblem of strength and unyielding resistance."[25] A proclamation setting forth the justification and purposes of the revolution was prepared, but before the new government could get under way, July 10, 1846, the American flag was officially sent to Sonoma.

The nearly simultaneous development of the Bear Flag force and the appearance of the U.S. troops in the north and south made for a monumental confusion in the Mexican province of California.

"Commodore John Drake Sloat, commander of the United States naval forces in the Pacific, had only recently raised the stars and stripes over the California capital of Monterey. A short two weeks after Sloat's successful conquest, Commodore Robert Stockton arrived from far-off

---

[24]Dr. Platon M. Vallejo, Memoirs of the Vallejos, 1914, Page 21.
[25]Simeon Ide, The Conquest of California by the Bear Flag Party, Rio Grande Press, Inc. (diary), Page 47.

Virginia and assumed command of all American forces in California.

Stockton, a man of action, wasted little time in occupying the California communities of San Diego and Los Angeles, two of the last strongholds under Mexican rule. Meeting little opposition, Stockton assumed all conquests complete and placed Captain Gillespie in command as he sailed for his Monterey headquarters."[26]

The war was over and the treaty of Guadalupe Hidalgo was signed on February 2, 1848. "Six flags flew over California before the American conquest came in 1846. The flag of Spain was the first, for she discovered the area in 1542, erected the first mission and presidio there in 1769, and ruled until 1822. Prior to actual Spanish settlement, Sir Francis Drake had raised the English standard at Nova Albion in 1579. From 1809 to 1841 the flag of the Russian American Company flew over several posts north of San Francisco Bay. The pirate Hippolyto Bouchard sacked the capital at Monterey in 1818 and hoisted the flag of Buenos Aires. The Mexican ensign warily guarded the turbulent territory from 1822 to 1846. The Bear Flag of the California Republic was the sixth to fly over California before the United States flag was officially unfurled atop the custom house at Monterey."[27]

Now, after six eras, each with its own flag flying over California soil, the American flag would fly over the farms, the valleys, and the hills hiding the vast reserves of gold. It would not be long before California was known as the land of gold.

---

[26]Randall A. Reinstedr, Portraits of the Past, Monterey Savings and Loan Association, 1979, Page 10.
[27]Simeon Ide, The Conquest of California by the Bear Flag Party, Rio Grande Press, Inc., (diary), Page 6.

Sebastian Viscaino wrote, 300 years before the gold rush of 1849, back to the king of Spain. He told the king that the natives of California were well acquainted with minerals from the earth, especially gold and silver. Later many tales have produced rumors that gold existed in California, but it wasn't until 1841 that a verified story surfaced. The native gold dust was found on the San Francisco ranch, 45 miles north-westerly from Los Angels City, in June, 1841. The gold was found in an area drained by the Santa Clara River, "from a point some fifteen or twenty miles from its mouth to its source, and easterly beyond Mount San Bernardino."[28]

An early California pioneer, J.J. Warner, who arrived in the state in 1831, wrote in his historical review of Los Angeles County that the gold was found by Francisco Lopez, a native of California, in March 1842, at San Francisquito, about 35 miles northwest of Los Angeles. The circumstances of the discovery by Lopez, as related by Lopez himself, are as follows: "Lopez, with a companion, was out in search of some stray horses, and about midday they stopped under some trees and tied their horses out to feed, they resting under the shade, when Lopez, with his sheath-knife, dug up some wild onions, and in the dirt discovered a piece of gold, and, searching further, found some more. He brought these to town, and showed them to his friends, who at once declared there must be a place of gold. This news being circulated, numbers of citizens went to the place, and commenced prospecting in the neighborhood, and found it to be a fact that there was a placer of gold."[29]

---

[28]History of State of California and Biographical Record of San Joaquin County, San Joaquin County, 1909, Page 155.
[29]Ibid., Page 155.

Colonel Warner says, "The news of this discovery soon spread among the inhabitants from Santa Barbara to Los Angeles, and in a few weeks hundreds of people were engaged in washing and winnowing the sands and earth of these gold fields. From these mines was obtained the first parcel of California gold dust received at the United States Mint in Philadelphias, and which was sent with Alfred Robinson, and went in a merchant ship around Cape Horn. This shipment of gold was 18.34 ounces before and 18.1 ounces after melting; fineness .925; value, $344.75, or over $19 to the ounce, a very superior quality of gold dust. It was deposited in the mint July 8, 1843.'"[30]

Also in question is the exact date of discovery of gold at Coloma in January 1848. For many years the Associated Pioneers of the Territorial Days of California held an annual dinner to celebrate the anniversary of the discovery on January 18th. Members of this organization were all in California on the day that Marshall picked up the first nuggets in the millrace. Later celebrations were held on January 24th. The Associated Pioneers later protested the shift in dates.

On the morning of discovery, John Marshall had shut off the water and had walked down the tailrace to see what gravel and debris had been washed away during the night. He was attempting to cut the millrace deeper by using the water power, which would be used to power the sawmill. Seeing the reflection on a bright pebble, he picked it up and realized that it was some type of mineral. By striking the pebble with a rock he ascertained that it was malleable; and he knew it was gold. Because Sutter had failed to send supplies to Marshall and his crew, Marshall had to go down to Sutter's Fort. On the trip down to the fort, he picked up some more gold in a ravine, which later became known as Mormon Island, a rich gold location. The news took two months to reach San Francisco,

---

[30]Ibid., Page 156.

21

but the great emotional gold rush was not in progress until the middle of May 1848, four months later.

"Captain Sutter had almost 40 Mormons in his employ at the two places. We know the names of six Mormons who were at the sawmill at the moment gold was discovered: Alexander Stephens, James S. Brown, James Barger, William Johnston, Azariah Smith and Henry W. Bigler. In all there are only twenty-seven Mormon names which can be traced as workers at the flour mill."[31]

Henry Bigler's Journal, in which he writes, explains that great role in history of the Mormon Battalion and how they happened upon the greatest historical event in the history of California. The Mormon Battalion was broken up after they had been paid in Los Angeles on July 19, 1847; some of the soldiers decided to re-enlist, but the rest went up the San Pedro River about 3 miles and got organized to move to Beare River Valley. After intending on going east by the way of Walker's Pass, they changed their minds and decided to travel to Sutter's Fort; they got some of their animals shod at the blacksmith shop that Sutter had built. Traveling on, they met Sam Brannan who had come down from Salt Lake to meet the party and to deliver them instructions. On September 14, 1847, Captain Sutter offered employment to all of the Mormon party. The diary of Hittell for Sept. 17, 1847 reads, "All hand was on the ditch with spades, plows, picks, shovels, and few scrapers. [In the evening they found that each man had earned $1.50.]"[32]

Hittel's diary entry for September 27 painted this picture. "A man drest in buckskin came to our quarters while we were at dinner informing us that Captain Sutter wanted 4 men from

---

[31]Reva Stanley, Sutter's Mormon Workmen at Natoma and Coloma in 1848, California Historical Society Quarterly, September 1935, Vol. 14, Page 269.
[32]Ibid., Page 273.

our crowd to go with him (the man in buckskin) up the American Fork into the mountains about 30 miles to work and help build a saw mill. This man who we were to accompany was James W. Marshall, an entire stranger to us but proved to be a gentlemen nevertheless. He told us that he had been up in the mountains with a few hands only short time but as some of them were going to leave soon he wished to get a few more. We learnt that he and Sutter were in co-partnership in building the sawmill. So late that afternoon myself and three others [Hittell version: Israel Evans, Azariah Smith and William Johnson] sat out with Mr. Marshall accompanied by Mr. Charles Bennet.] There I found several of the battalion boys who had remained at Sutters at the time our company past there in August. Four however soon left and returned to the fort and went to work on Sutters Flouring Mill."[33]

Henry Bigler's Journal tells a slightly different version of the gold discovery. "My Journal tells me it was on the afternoon of the 24th day of January 1848 while I was at my drill busy preparing to put in a blast when Marshall as usual went to see Wimmer and the Indians who were at work towards the lower end of the race, when he sent a young Indian for Brown to send him a plate. At this time Brown and one of the Indians were whip sawing in the millyard. Brown gave the Indian the plate just before we quit work and he came up and said he believed he had found a gold mine. He did not show us anything neither did he say he had any but went off up to his own house on the side of the mountain but before we went to bed he came in and commenced talking with us saying he believed he had found gold near the lower end of the race and if I remember rite he told us that he tried to melt some and could not do it. He spoke to Brown and me saying, 'Brown I want you and Bigler to shut down the head gate early in the morning, throw in a little saw dust, rotten leaves and dirt and make all tight and I'll see what there is in the morning.' Accordingly the next morning we done as he told us while

---

[33]Ibid., Page 273.

Marshall went alone down into the race and we went in for our breakfast and after we had breakfasted and came out, Marshall came up carrying his old white hat in his arm looking wonderfully pleased and good natured. There was a heavy smile on his countenance. Some of the boys said they knew in a minute as soon as they seen him that something was the matter. As he came up he said, 'Boys, by god, I believe I have found a gold mine' and sat his hat on the work bench that stood in the mill yard. Every man gathered instantly around to see what he had and there sure enough, on the top of the hat crown (knocked in a little) lay the pure stuff. How much I do not know, perhaps half an ounce, maybe more from the smallest particles up to the size of a kernel of wheat or larger. The most of it was in very thin small flakes.

Every man fully experts his conviction believing firmly it was gold although none of us had ever seen gold before in its native state. Azariah Smith pulled out a five dollar piece (part of his soldier money) and we compared the dust with it. There seemed to be no difference as to color or weight only that the coin looked a little the brightest and rather more white. This we accounted for because of the alloy in it. Two or three days afterwards Marshall said he would take what gold we had found and go down to the Fort and have it tested, saying to us at the same time to keep it to ourselves until we knew what it was. He was gone four days and when he returned and was asked what it was his reply was, 'Oh boy, By God, it is the pure stuff.'"[34]

As one would expect, all work ceased on the sawmill and Sutter's employees prospected for gold. Most of the Mormon Battalion gathered at Mormon Island and found more very rich gold deposits. In early April, the Willis boys, one or possibly two, left their mining and went to the Fort; they probably went to Yerba Buena, later known as San Francisco,

---

[34]Ibid., Page 274.

and told Sam Brannan about the secret gold discovery. Mr. Brannan, at the time, was publishing a little newspaper at Yerba Buena named the California Star; he published the news about the gold strike on the south fork of the American River. The gold rush, which would ruin Captain Sutter and leave John Marshall a poor man, was on in full force; the treasure-seekers would rush in from every continent. "The excitement produced was intense; the blacksmith dropped his hammer, the carpenter his plane, the mason his trowel, the farmer has sickle, the baker his loaf, the tapster his bottle."[35]

General William Tecumseh Sherman found the following scene when he toured the gold fields. "About noon we reached Coloma, the place where gold had been first discovered. The hills were higher, and the timber of better quality. The river was narrower and golder, and but few miners were at work there, by reason of Marshall's and Sutter's claim to the site. There stood the saw-mill unfinished, the dam and tail-race just as they were left when the Mormons ceased work. Marshall and his family and wife and half a dozen tow-head children were there, guarding their supposed treasure; living in a house made of clapboards. Here also we were shown many specimens of gold, of a coarser grain than that found at Mormon Island. The next day we crossed the American River to its north side, and visited many small camps of men, in what were called the 'dry diggings.' Little pools of water stood in the beds of the streams, and these were used to wash the dirt; and there the gold was in every conceivable shape and size, some of the specimens weighing several ounces. Some of the diggings were extremely rich, but as a whole they were more precarious in results than in the river. Sometimes a lucky fellow would hit on a 'pocket' and collect several thousand dollars in a few days, and then again he would be shifting about from place to place, 'prospecting', and spending all he had made, Little stores were being opened at every point,

---

[35]Reverand Walter Colton U.S.N., Three Years in California [diary recopied], 1949, Page 246.

where flour, bacon, etc., were sold; everything being a dollar a pound and a meal usually costing three dollars. Nobody paid for a bed, for he slept on the ground, without fear of cold or rain."[36]

In his diary, Reverend Colton wrote about a group of prospectors who worked on the Feather River. "They employed about thirty wild Indians who are attached to the rancho owned by one of the party. They worked precisely seven weeks and three days, and have divided seventy-six thousand eight hundred and forty-four dollars, nearly eleven thousand dollars to each."[37]

[36]General William Tecumseh Sherman, Recollections of California 1846-1861, 1945, Page 42.
[37]Reverend Walter Colton U.S.N., Three Years in California [diary recopied], 1949, Page 252.

An air of excitement soon hit anyone who came in contact with the news of the discovery. On June 1, 1848, Thomas Oliver Larkin wrote the Secretary of State in Washington, D.C. regarding the news of the discovery. He wrote from San Francisco, Upper California after Governor Mason requested Larkin to look into the matter of the estate of a large property owned with a lot of indebtedness. Larkin wrote,

"I leave here today for the Sacramento River. I have to report to the State Department one of the most astonishing excitements and state of affairs now existing in this country that perhaps has ever been brought to the notice of Government. On the American Fork of the Sacramento and Feather River, another branch of the same and adjoining lands, there has been within the present year discovered a placer, a vast tract of land containing gold in small particles. This gold thus far has been taken on the banks of the river from the surface to eighteen inches in depth and is supposed deeper and to extend over the country. On account of the convenience of washing, the people have to this time only gathered the metal on the banks, which is done simply with a shovel, filling a shallow dish, bowl, basket, or tin pan with a quantity of black sand similar to the class used on paper and washing out the sand by movement of the vessel. It is now two or three weeks since the men employed in these washings have appeared in this town with gold to exchange for merchandise and provisions. I presume near twenty thousand dollars (20,000$) of this gold has as yet been so exchanged.

Some two or three hundred of the men have remained up the river or are gone to their homes for the purpose of returning to the Placers and washing immediately with shovels, picks and baskets, many of them for the first few weeks depending on borrowing from others. I have seen the written statement of the work of one man for sixteen days, which average twenty five ($25) dollars

per day. Others have with a shovel and pan or wooden
bowl washed out ten to over fifty dollars per day. There
are now some men yet washing who have five
hundred to one thousand dollars. As they stand two
feet deep in the river, they work but a few hours in the
day and not every day of the week.

A few of the men have been down in boats to this port,
having twenty to thirty ounces of gold each, about three
hundred dollars (300$). I am confident that this town (San
Francisco) has one half of its tenements empty, locked
up with the furniture. The owners - store keepers,
lawyers, mechanics and labourers - all gone to Sacramento
with their families. Small parties of five to fifteen men
have sent to this town and offered cooks ten to fifteen
dollars per day for a few weeks. Mechanics and teamsters
earning the year past five to eight dollars per day have
struck and gone. Several U.S. Volunteers have deserted.
U.S. barque Anita, belonging to the Army, now at anchor
here, has but six men. One Sandwich Island vessel in
port lost all her men. Common spades and shovels,
one month ago worth one dollar, will now bring ten dollars
at the gold regions."[38]

As the word and the rumors of extravagance spread,
men started for the easy wealth of El Dorado. Surprisingly,
ships loaded with would-be miners arrived from as far away as
Chile. The setting, they discovered on their arrival, was far
from what they imagined. A medical doctor from Chile received
no calls for his services. He wrote home, "Few people become
ill, and even fewer seemed to fear death. With no income, the
price the doctor had to pay for supplies seemed exorbitant.
Only coffee, beans, and meat were cheap, the latter selling for
25 cents a pound. Cheese, raisins, figs, if obtainable, cost
$1.00 a pound, butter $1.25. The price of this flour, imported
from Chile, fluctuated daily. Flour on one ship might sell for
$30.00 a barrel, and while it was being unloaded, another ship
might arrive from Chile causing the price to drop as low as $9.

---

[38]Thomas Oliver Larkin, The Larkin Papers, Vol. VII,
1847-1848, 1960, Page 285.

Supercargoes complained that North American businessmen would bid eagerly against one another for a ship's entire cargo and repudiate the agreement when another shipload of flour arrived."[39] Some enterprising leaders brought gangs of laborers to do the actual mining for them while they sat back and got wealthy. Often the laborers quickly forgot their promises and accepted work in San Francisco at fantastic wages, which would double in the spring when the mining would open up. "Few Chileans were carpenters, but they did know how to lay adobe blocks and soon got jobs as bricklayers. Most of the men had, since childhood, watched their mothers bake bread in outdoor beehive ovens and, in San Francisco, they quickly found employment as bakers."[40]

A Chilean doctor wrote home about his fascination with

"the abundance of gold in so many persons' hands. Workmen in the street would pour a sparkling little stream of gold from a dirty leather poke into a friend's callused palm. In shops the precious dust was poured on scales in payment for a few groceries, or a pinch was bestowed as a tip for some minor service. Everyone seemed to have gold and everyone talked constantly about the certainty of years."[41]

The newcomers to California soon learned of the dangers. They had to get from San Francisco to the gold fields. Travel was not safe unless one was in groups of 25 or more. In addition to the problems posed by the Indians, bears, and diseases such as typhoid, yellow fever and anemia were a problem. The first portion of the journey could be by boat up the Sacramento River, but only if one had the money to purchase the fare. The last part of the trip necessitated

---

[39]Jay Monaghan, Chile, Peru, and The California Gold-rush of 1849, 1973, Page 127.
[40]Ibid., Page 128.
[41]Ibid., Page 129.

carrying one's belongings on his back and walking 30 to 60 miles.

Many of the vessels that carried miners from Chile to San Francisco returned without a cargo of men; instead they came back loaded with gold and the motivation for others to follow the cry for gold. "Ship after ship arrived in Valparaiso from California with more gold. In one period of six days, three vessels brought 3,533 ounces of dust. This amounted to approximately $60,000 of currency in addition to the $2500 that was often spent every day in Valparaiso by passengers coming ashore from north-bound vessels. So large an inflow completely upset the economy of a town of 30,000."[42]

Stories of immense wealth, and the ease with which it was acquired, continually circulated in Valparaiso.

> "California gold had become commonplace in Valparasio, and merchants often attracted customers by displaying unusually shaped nuggets. El Mercurio [the local newspaper], under the heading PEPITA MONSTRUO DE ORO, announced that a person recently returned from California had brought back a chunk of quartz the size and shape of a human foot, laced throughout with gold. This curiosity, on display in a store on Calle del Cabo, weighed 90 ounces and cost the owner $1,200 in San Francisco. Many North Americans on their way to California saw their first gold in Valparaiso and purchased samples of it to keep as relics. Later gold in another form, also a novelty, soon appeared in Valparaiso. Gold eagles, minted in San Francisco, became accepted currency in town. Also, in circulation were United States half eagles, which were described as being slightly smaller and thicker than a Chilean half ounce."[43]

The shipping records show that 303 ships sailed out of Valparaiso for California in 1849.

---

[42]James Melville Gilliss, Chile: Its Geography, Climate, 1855, Page 229.
[43]Ibid., Page 229.

The first word of the discovery of gold in California reached Brooklyn on October 4, 1848 when the Brooklyn Eagle reported that a great rush were preparing to leave after hearing rumors of rich gold deposits. The paper predicted that 50,000 people would leave within the next few months. On the same day they reported that 6 ships in New York and 3 from Boston were loading for California. On December 14, 1848 the paper listed 31 vessels at New York, 9 at Philadelphia, and a half dozen at both Boston and Baltimore preparing to leave for San Francisco.

By December 18, 1848 a miner, Joseph H. Cutting, returned to New Orleans with $1500 of gold that he picked up using a pick-axe, a shovel, butcher's knife, and a pan. He had been in California a year, but spent only 42 days in the gold region.

The first letter back to Brooklyn explaining the lack of gold coins on the West Coast was printed in the Daily Eagle on January 22, 1849. Is this letter, which was written on August 23, 1848, what prompted Hiram Norris to get the dies carved for his 1849 gold coin?

By late July, 1849, the news was back in Brooklyn that a favorite son, and friend of the editor of the Brooklyn Daily Eagle, was coining money in Benicia. The article read: "At work. -we see that our friend Norris, who went out to California in February last, has established himself at Benicia and is engaged in coining the gold of California into quarter and half Eagles. - His half eagles bear the initials of the firm in New York to which he belongs: 'Norris Greig and Norris.' Mr. Norris is a brother of Rev. Mr. Norris of the Sands street Methodist church and went from this city." [44]

The newspaper of August 1, 1849 brought more relevant news. It reported:

---

[44]Brooklyn Daily Eagle, July 30, 1849, Page 3.

31

"California Coin. 'We mentioned a day or two ago
that Mr. Hiram Norris, of the firm of Norris, Greig & Norris,
New York, had commenced the business of coining
gold at Benicia. Yesterday we had a sight of one of the
coins. It is of a brighter yellow htan our own coin, and
contains no allow, being entirely pure. On one side
is the American Eagle, and encircling it the words,
California gold without alloy.' On the other side, in the
centre, is the date. '1849,' and around it the words,
'Full weigh of half eagle. N.G.&N., (initials of the
    firm) San Francisco.' We understand that Mr. Norris
coined several thousand dollars before
    the steamersailed." [45]

---

[45]Brooklyn Daily Eagle, August 1, 1849, Page 2.

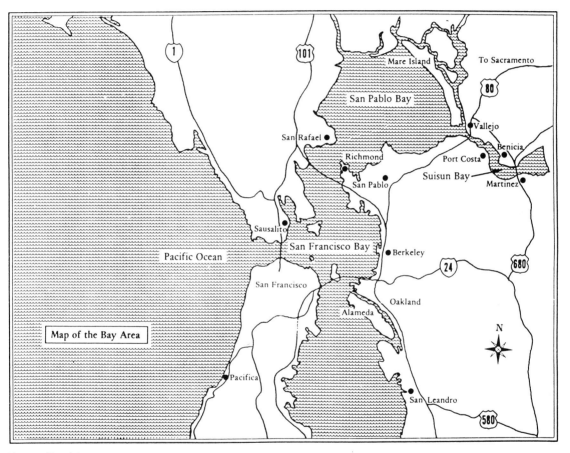

Figure 1. Map of the Bay Area.

A SNAPSHOT OF MINING

The great gold fountain of the Pacific Coast poured forth its riches from many varied regions of the state of California. The auriferous strata were so varied that many different methods of mining the earth were very necessary; what would work in harvesting the alluvial deposits was totally different from the techniques that would mine the underground deposits.

No matter what the methods necessitated, they were sure to be developed because of the tremendous wealth and the gold fever that the gold created. George Tinkham wrote, "Cornelius Sullivan and his companions at this time were on their way from Monterey to Coloma. In camp one night a Spaniard came along and said, 'Oh, my friends, there is lots of gold, chunks as big as my fist, on the Stanislaus.' The party then turned from Coloma to Jamestown. 'Never will I forget the impressions of the scene before us,' said Sullivan to the writer. 'Under a brushwood tent supported by upright poles sat James D. Savage, measuring that pouring gold dust into the candle boxes by his side. Five hundred or more naked Indians, with belts of cloth bound around their waists or suspended from their heads brought the dust to Savage, and in return for it received a bright cloth or some beads.'"[46]

In May, 1850 the Stockton Times reported some huge nuggets. "Mr. J.J. Holliday this morning favoured me with the inspections of a lump of gold, nearly pure, weighing 7 lbs. 9 oz., found by Mr. A. Ford (of Morgan county, Missouri) at Cuyota Creek, a tributary of the Stanislaus, one of the nearest rivers to Stockton. Messr. Douglas & Rankin have in their possession a lump of gold weighing 9 lbs. 1 oz. found at Agua Frio. We have seen it."[47]

---

[46]George Henry Tinkham, California Men & Events, 1915, Page 79.
[47]Stockton Times (newspaper), May 10, 1850, Page 1.

The miners' methods ranged from very primitive, in the beginning, to complex as the gold got more difficult to reach. At first baskets or basins of willow twigs were utilized to hold the gold picked up by hand; a common sheath-knife would be used to pry the nuggets out of the chispas. The use of the common gold-pan followed the use of the Spanish-American batea, or bowl; both of these devices would use a rotary motion to separate the gold from the sand and gravel. If the gold bearing earth was not next to a creek, the material was often carried to water's edge. "Chinese Diggings in Tuolumne County was an instance of this. Here were seen troops of sturdy Chinese groaning along under the weight of huge sacks of earth brought to the surface from a depth of eighteen feet, and deposited in heaps, after a weary tramp, along banks of a muddy pool. There were washed by other parties stationed there for the purpose, and the day's proceeds equally divided. At Shaw's Flat, at the time of its discovery, similar means were used."[48]

Some Mexicans used a method of pulverizing the mud and sand, pick out the pebbles, place the mixture on a heavy cloth and toss the earth up in the air and let the breeze carry away the waste. The cradle was soon invented; it was a box about 3 or 4 feet long which was rocked back and forth. Water was added to wash away the debris. The "long tom" was over 10 feet long, and earth and water would be added to the elevated end; at the bottom and box with cleats would catch the gold as it fell from the long box. At a place called Murderer's Bar, the miners even attempted to change the course of the river, so that the water flow was out of the way so the old stream-bed could be worked.

Because the specific gravity of gold is superior, the gold particles work their way down to a layer of rock, often bed-rock. A method of exploration, when the gold was found at depth, in

---

[48]William V. Wells, How We Gt Gold in California, 1860, Page 7.

35

California was called coyoteing, or drifting. Passages through the rock and clay were found thirty or forty feet below the surface. Once the coyote was completed, the upper earth did not have to be shoveled away. Tallow candles were used to light the areas. These arched passages would only be waist high and sometimes had to be supported by timbers. The miners later wrote of honeycombing an area of twenty acres in six months.

Some miners, particularly those acquainted with methods in Mexico, used the horse-pulled 'rastra.' "Beside the quartz-mill proper, driven with water or steam power, there is the primitive Spanish-American rastra, or drag, which we saw in operation in Bear Valley, in Maripose County, and other places."[49]

Later, as the search turned to mountain-sides and canyons, lode mining took over as the main technique to free the gold. Various systems of shafts and tunnels were devised. The tunnel near the town of Sonora went into volcanic rock a distance of fifteen-hundred feet. To avoid the costly pick and shovel work, hoses and giant nozzles came into play by April 1852; the water pressure would wash away the over-burden exposing the gold-bearing clays.

General Sherman, on a tour of the region, explained the scene. "In this valley is a flat, or gravel-bed, which in high water is an island, or is overflown, but at the time of our visit was simply a level gravel-bed of the river. On its edges men were digging and filling buckets with the finer earth and gravel, which was carried to a machine like a baby's cradle, open at the foot and at the head a plate of sheet-iron or zinc, punctured full of holes. On this metallic plate was emptied the earth, and after was then poured on it from buckets, while one man shook the cradle with violent rocking by a handle. On the bottom were nailed cleats of wood. With this rude machine four men

---

[49]Ibid., Page 18.

could earn from forty to one hundred dollars a day, averaging sixteen dollars, or a gold ounce, per man per day. While the sun blazed down on the heads of the miners with tropical heat, the water was bitter cold, and all hands were either standing in the water or had their clothes wet all the time; yet there were no complaints of rheumatism or cold. We made our camp on a small knoll, a little below the island, and from it could overlook the busy scene. A few bush-huts nearby served as stores, boarding-houses, and for sleeping; but all hands slept on the ground,with pine-leaves and blankets for bedding. As soon as the news spread that the Governor was there, persons came to see us, and volunteered all kinds of information, illustrating it by samples of the gold, which was a uniform kind, "scale-gold", bright and beautiful. A large variety, of every conceivable shape and form, was found in the smaller gulches round about, but the gold in the river-bed was uniformly "scale-gold." I remember that Mr. Clark was in camp talking to Colonel Mason about matters and things generally."[50]

The Stockton Times wrote about the great wealth, and how one had to go to depths to retrieve it. "The mines to which we particularly allude are exhaustless; we can come to no other conclusion. Mr. Mahan, of Sonora, informs us that the placer which is now the site of Columbia City, has been dug to a depth of sixty-two feet; that gold was struck four feet from the surface, and was taken in small and large quantities thence to the bottom of the excavation; that miners in many instances have taken out four and five pounds of the precious metal each in one day; that on Friday last a lump of pure gold, weighing four pounds and seven ounces, was discovered; and that it is now the general belief that every flat and gulch of the river Tualumne is equally richly impregnated with the precious metal."[51]

---

[50]General William Tecumseh Sherman, Recollections of California 1846-1861, reproduced 1945 by Joseph A. Sullivan.
[51]Stockton Times (newspaper), May 11, 1850, Page 2.

As a result of the hours, day, and weeks of toil and back-breaking work in tunnels and icy waters, a colossal genre of tales was produced in addition to the treasure trove of gold. Many of these were humorous, while others told of tragedy and suffering. The lure of gold left behind humorous situations as domestic society was turned inside out. Edwin Corle wrote in 1849, "The old fever has reached every servant in Monterey; none are trusted in their engagement beyond a week, and as for compulsion, it is like attempting to drive fish into a net with ocean before them. Gen. Mason, Lieut. Lanman, and myself, form a mess; we have a house and all the table furniture and culinary apparatus requisite; but our servants have run, one after another, till we are almost in despair: even Sambo, who we thought would stick by from laziness, if no other cause, ran last night; and this morning, for the fortieth time, we had to take to the kitchen, and cook our own breakfast. A general of the United States Army, a commander of a man-of-war, and the Alcalde of Monterey, in a smoking kitchen, grinding coffee, toasting a herring and pealing onions. Another tale of change: Another bag of gold from the mines and another spasm in the community. It was brought down by a sailor from Yuba River, and contains a hundred and thirty-six ounces. It is the most beautiful gold that has appeared in the market. My carpenters, at work on the school-house, on seeing it, threw down their saws and planes, shouldered their picks, and are off for the Yuba. Three seamen ran from the 'Warren', forfeiting their four years' pay; and a whole platoon of soldiers from the fort left only their colors behind. One old woman declared she would never again break an egg or kill a chicken, without examining yolk and gizzard."[52]

The Reverend and Alcalde Walter Colton of Monterey also gave up his position and joined the gold-seekers. A week after leaving his home and responsibilities he wrote in his diary, "I met a man today from the mines in patched buckskins, rough as a badger from his hole, who had fifteen thousand

---

[52]Edwin Cole, The Royal Highway, 1849, Page 247.

dollars in yellow dust, swung at his back. Talk to him of brooches, gold-headed canes, and Carpenter's coats! Why he can unpack a lump of gold that would throw all Chestnut-street [Cotton is thinking Philadelphia] into spasms. And there is more where this came from."[53]

Unable to locate a claim which produced any gold, a young man wandered into a camp of successful miners. After hearing his tale of woe, one miner said, "Boys, he said, 'I'll work an hour for that chap yonder is you will.' The rest agreed, and at the end of the hour they turned over to the young man something like a hundred dollars in gold dust. They then made up a list of tools and told the boy, 'Now go and buy these tools and come back here. We'll stake out a good claim for you, and after that you'll paddle your own canoe!"[54]

Funerals were not exempt from gold-field humor. A miner died on Carson Creek and the other miners decided to hold services for the departed. Frank Marryat described the scene, "A miner of the neighborhood, who had the reputation of having been a prominent and powerful preacher in the eastern states, was called upon to officiate; and he consented to do so. After assembling and taking 'drinks all around' the party proceeded with becoming gravity to the grave, which had been dug at a distance of about a hundred yards from the camp. When the spot was reached and the body lowered, the minister commenced an extempore prayer, while the crowd reverently fell upon their knees. For a while all went well; but the prayer was unnecessarily long and at last some of the congregation began, in abstracted way to finger the loose earth that had been thrown up from the grave. It proved to be thick with gold, and an excitement was immediately apparent in the kneeling crowd. Upon this the preacher stopped and inquiringly asked, 'Boys, what's that?' took a view of the ground for himself, and as he did so, shouted, 'Gold! Gold! - and the richest kind of

---

[53]Ibid., Page 248.
[54]Joseph Henry Jackson, Anybody's Gold, 1941, Page 82.

diggings!' The congregation is dismissed!' The dead miner was taken from his auriferous grave to be buried elsewhere, while the funeral party, with the minister at their head, lost no time in prospecting and staking out new diggings."[55]

Sometimes luck just wasn't with a prospector; James H. Carson, after whom Carson Creek was named, had his luck turn from fantastic to poor. He and several associates took 180 ounces of gold each out of Carson Creek in ten days in 1848. He abandoned his next diggings, but made a huge mistake in leaving the area. "He should have walked a few hundred feet up the hill. There was a man named Hance, following a straying mule, saw yellow metal in an outcropping of quartz. With a rock he knocked off a chunk of gold weighing fourteen pounds. That was in 1850, less than two years after Carson's original discovery and abandonment of the district. That became the world-famous Morgan Mine. A single blast there, according to such unimpeachable authority as J. Ross Browne, knocked down one hundred and ten thousand dollars worth of gold. Colonel Morgan took from a hole twelve feet long, six feet wide, and nine feet deep, over five millions of dollars."[56]

Other riches were overlooked, even in the most unlikely of places. The San Joaquin Republican announced on October 4, 1851, that workmen were digging a well in a jail yard right in San Francisco; the lot was on Broadway between Kearney and Dupont Streets. The paper went on to say that pieces of quartz with particles of gold were found at a depth of fifty feet and that the rock sample was being analyzed by Moffat & Co.

The amount of wealth that left the gold fields is staggering. Daniel Coit wrote a letter from Mexico City on November 8, 1848, stating that he had purchased some gold

---

[55]Ibid., Page 83.
[56]C.B. Glasscock, A Gold Highway, 1934, Page 276.

dust in Mexico; he had purchased $30,000 of gold from an American. "He, with another American, had been some time in the country engaged in farming operations. Hearing the extraordinary reports of the gold mines, they determined (he and his partner) to take Indians whom they had in their employ, some thirty in number, and proceed with them to the gold district to try their hand at the business. So great is the value of labor, owing to the facility with which every man can collect gold for himself, that they agreed to find their Indians and pay them besides $2 per day. The result of the undertaking was that these two Americans, at the expiration of only six weeks time, divided $60,000."[57]

Very early in the gold rush the tremendous wealth that would be taken home was readily apparent. Coit wrote, "He says Governor Mason, well known in the United States, has traversed the whole of the gold region and says that about $35,000 in value (estimating the gold at $16 per ounce) is collected daily, or at the rate of upwards of $10,000,000 per anum."[58] Governor Mason wrote a letter dated August 17, 1848 to Secretary of State Buchanan confirming the account of Coit.

A Lieut. Loeser arrived in New Orleans aboard the Falcon and was proudly showing his nuggets to citizens of that city by December 5, 1848. The Washington Union paper confirmed Loeser's arrival. "We readily admit that the account so nearly approached the miraculous that we were relieved by the evidence of our own senses on the subject. The specimens have all the appearance of the native gold we had seen from the mines of North Carolina and Virginia; and we are informed that the secretary will send the small chest of gold to the mint, to be melted into coin and bars."[59]

---

[57]Daniel Coit, Digging For Gold Without a Shovel 1848-1851, Oregon Historical Quarterly No. 4, Page 56.
[58]Ibid., Page 57.
[59]Hubert Howe Bancroft, History of California, Vol. XXIII, Vol. 6

Not only was gold leaving California for Mexico, New Orleans, and the East Coast, but it was also going home to Oregon by those prospectors returning to their farms with their new-found wealth. The huge size of the shipments is illustrated in the newspaper, "IMMENSE SHIPMENT OF GOLD DUST by the Oregon - Today the largest amount of gold dust will be carried from our shores ever before known at one shipment. The amount entered on the manifest of the steamer Oregon, Pearson, commander, is computed at two millions, of which the house of Adams & Co., alone, enter at least six hundred thousand. The receipt of this immense amount of treasure in New York will, it is believed, tend to revive the drooping state of the finances of our distance speculating neighbors of the Atlantic states. The house of Burgoyne & Co. forwarded $300,000. We have been unable to learn the amounts forwarded by the other banking houses in our city. The Oregon will sail this afternoon, at 6 o'clock, from Long Wharf."[60]

1848-1859, Page 116.
[60]San Joaquin Republican (newspaper), October 14, 1851, Page 1.

The California gold-rush created an entirely new set of needs for a generation of men far from the comforts of home and readily available supplies and services. The needs, which were as varied as the towns and cities from which the miners came, were both physical and emotional. Especially for some of the younger gold-seekers, the loss of home was powerful. "California miners were periodically troubled by homesickness. 'We talk often about home and friends, but if ever we see them again or not is the question, and then when and how. Are my brothers and sisters all alive and well yet, I ask myself often.' As time passed and the small amount of gold in the pouch began to disappear, most miners like Windeler, were forced to buy their essential supplies and food each week on credit, and hope to obtain enough gold in the next five or six days' work to pay their bills and obtain credit for the following week. Many fell behind in their payments and if a lucky strike was made the honest miner's first thought was to pay his debts to maintain his credit rating. Most men came to realize that they just couldn't go back home and do something, for I am afraid that I will spoil myself here and get sick and lame."[61]

Of greater, and more immediate need, was the need for survival in a land that had been stolen from the native inhabitants. The early problems in the Yosemite Valley illustrate the urgency. "I have seen men ride into town with their clothes stuck full of arrows. I recall Colonel Owen, he was attacked five miles out, riding up a mountain; at first flight of arrows, his mule whirled suddenly, throwing his carbine from the pommel of his saddle, where it was hanging; he used his two revolvers as long as they held out and then depended

---

[61]Adolphus Windeler, The California Gold Rush Diary of a German Sailor, Edited by W. Turrentine Jackson, 1969, Page 21.

upon his mule for the chances. There were three arrows in the mule's flanks, five in Owen's clothing and one in his hat, but only one drew blood. He did not know how many of his shots took effect, but felt sure that some of the attackers did not get away with whole skins."[62]

As important in a miner's life as homesickness, was medical treatment. "The typical miner was continuously plagued by illness. Doctors were scarce and very hard to find in an emergency. Windeler expressed sympathy for his partner: 'Theodor has been laid up 6 days with a swelling in his jawbone. Today he got mad and hit himself a lick on the place which broke the abscess and now he can talk again. Hard for a man to be sick, didn't know what to do.' The hard work, poor housing, and inadequate diet took their toll and the California miner found himself physically exhausted and chronically ill after one or two seasons of hard work. Windeler was no exception. 'I felt very bad had the gripes like fury, so I had to send for some whiskey and pepper which I took with hot water then vomited...Got a hot stone to lay on my belly and so after a while I felt easier. Sam got me a dose of caster oil, which cured me up again, but I felt rather weak at night.'"[63]

Another great need was the desire to receive mail from home. The government was very slow to adjust their mail services to the needs of the miner. The job was doubly difficult because of the rapid movement of the miners from one prospect hole to the next, at the same time it was impossible for the working miner to travel to San Francisco to pick up his mail from the ships. To fill this gap private express services soon came into being to distribute the mail. Newspapers were also a luxury. "Bayard Taylor arrived in San Francisco with

---

[62]Newell D. Chamberlain, Call of Gold, Valley Publishers, 1977, Page 18.
[63]Adolphus Windeler, The California Gold Rush Diary of a German Sailor, Edited by W. Turrentine Jackson, 1969, Page 20.

another New Yorker who brought along 1,500 copies of New York newspapers in his baggage. As soon as he landed he began hawking his months-old newspapers in the streets. He disposed of all 1,500 at $1 apiece in two hours. Hearing of this I thought me of about a dozen papers which I had used to fill up crevices in packing my valise, wrote Taylor. There was a newspaper merchant at the corner of the City Hotel, and to him I proposed the sale of them, asking him to name a price. 'I shall want to make a good profit on the retail price', said he, and can't give more than ten dollars for the lot.' I was satisfied with the wholesale price, which was a gain of just four thousand per cent!" [64] Wells Fargo & Co. charged $5.00 to deliver a letter from San Francisco just to Benicia.

The hard-working newcomers had a constant need for laundry. The solutions to laundry, that we so take for granted, were difficult to find. Wyld's Guide to Prospective Immigrants to California described some possible solutions. "That is the greatest privation that a bachelor in this country is exposed to, Wyld's guide warned. Laundresses charged $5 to $8 to wash and press a dozen shirts and, even then, you have to court them besides, complained Wyld. Some men discarded their shirts when they became dirty; it was just as cheap to buy new ones. Others sent their dirty shirts to Hawaii and China. A vessel just in from Canton brought two hundred and fifty dozen; which had been sent out a few months before, wrote Bayard Taylor in 1850 while another from the Sandwich Islands [Hawaii] brought one hundred dozen, and the practice was becoming general.

Sending your shirts to a Chinese laundry that was actually in China may have been something to write home about, but it was no answer to the dirty clothes problem. By mid-1849, Mexican and Indian women were washing clothes

---

[64]Charles Lockwood, Suddenly San Francisco: The Early Years of an Instant City, San Francisco Examiner special project, 1978, Page 29.

out by the Presidio along the Fresh Pond, which soon became known as Washerwoman's Lagoon. They were doing so well that several dozen men set up laundries there too. Washing clothes may not have been traditionally a man's job, but it paid two or three times as much as pushing a wheelbarrow or unloading ships' cargoes.

"The washerwomen settled on one edge of the lagoon, and the washermen took over the other side. The men went into the business on a large scale, having their tents for ironing, their lare kettles for boiling the clothes, and their fluted washboards along the edge of the water," wrote the ever curious Bayard Taylor. It was an amusing sight to see a great, burly, long-bearded fellow kneeling on the ground, with sleeves rolled up to the elbows, and rubbing a shirt on the board with such violence that the sudes flew and the buttons, if there were any, must soon snap off. Their clearstarching and ironing were still more ludicrous, but, not withstanding, they succeeded fully as well as the women, and were rapidly growing rich from the profits of their business."[65]

Except in a few rare cases, mining tools were at a premium. "The Middle and North Fork of the American River were discovered by a few deserters, in September, where in the space of a few days they realized from five to twenty thousand dollars each; and they left California by the first conveyance. Tools for mining purposes were scarce and high; a pick, pan and shovel ranging from $50 to $200; butcher's knives from $10 to $25; while cradle washing machines from $200 to $800 each. Provisions were worth $2 per pound; woolen shirts $50 each; boots and shoes form $25 to $150 a pair."[66] Scales to weigh the gold were also needed. "The first scales for weighing gold were made by taking a piece of pine wood for the beam, pieces of sardine boxes for scales, and

---

[65]Ibid., Page 29.
[66]James H. Carson, Early Recollections of the Mines, San Joaquin Republican (newspaper), January 21, 1852, Page 1.

silver dollars for weights. Gold dust could even be purchased in any quantity at four and five-dollars per ounce in the diggings, and for six and eight dollars in the coast towns."[67] The Alta California was advertising, by May of 1849, many types of mining equipment; Thomas H. Winston had the following articles for sale at the city Hotel in San Francisco: "round pointed shovels, English spades, pick axes, gold washers, frying pans, axes, crowbars, hollow ware, mess chests, clothing, tents, tin ware; indeed every thing in quantity to traders and country merchants at lowest whole-sale prices, and to individuals at lowest retail prices. For sale for cash, or to good men on short time."[68] Tools were so hard to acquire that in September 1849, F. Morton rented a wheelbarrow for 32 days to a miner for $96.00.

Such basic needs as furniture had to be improvised. "Hove out our wing dam a fair way, then rigged our bedsteads. At dinner consisting of beans, had the hamb;berg on the stretch, talking about girls and their doings fixing our bedsteads each one made his to his own notion. Theodor made a willow wicker work, I made mine flat with elderbranches, Charley slung his hammock so every one sleeps as he likes best. Then came consideration about what to begin next."[69]

Conditions were so primitive at Hornitos that not one person had a watch or a clock. One of the miners remembered years later, "I made a sun dial on top of a stump to alignment of the north star and got noon hour very closely."[70]

---

[67]Ibid., Page 1.
[68]Alta California (newspaper), February 20, 1851, Page 3.
[69]Adolphus Windeler, The California Gold Rush Diary of a German Sailor, Edited by W. Turrentine Jackson, 1969, Page 68.
[70]Newell D. Chamberlain, Call of Gold, Valley Publishers, 1977, Page 21.

The mining camps had to continually improvise. Even in death, there weren't any easy remedies. A miner from Washington mine near Quartburgh wrote of the answer to the need for a casket. "When a miner died, we split a log in two, dug out the inside, like a mummy case, laid the body in it and pinioned it together with wooden pins."[71]

The availability of food differed from site to site; from mountain mining claims to the towns; it even differed from day to day. "At the close of 1848 our population consisted of about ten thousand. We promised to follow the miners to the towns on the coast, where about two-thirds had gone to winter; San Francisco, Monterey and Los Angeles had received the greater portion of this heterogeneous mass, men ragged and filthy in the extreme, with thousands of dollars in their pockets, filled the houses, and street, drinking and gambling away their piles. No supplies or accommodations could be obtained. In San Francisco in particular, every house and tent was nightly crowded with these beings, who were in many cases packed away in rooms like shad. I applied at a public house in San Francisco in October for food and lodgings- I got beef boiled, hard bread, and a cup of awful coffee, for which I paid the moderate sum of five dollars. By furnishing my own blankets and paying a dollar, I got permission to sleep on a bowling alley, after the rolling had ceased, which was near two o'clock in the morning."[72]

"In 1846 and '47, the price of the finest horses was $20; fat bullock, $6; wild mares 75 cents each; flour and vegetables - we didn't have any. We lived on beef and beans; beef dried, fried, roasted, boiled and broiled morning, noon, and night - as much as every man wanted - without money or price; with a change, at times, of elk, venison, and bear steak. The emigrants of 1846 did not expect to find any luxuries in

---

[71]Ibid., Page 21.
[72]James H. Carson, Early Recollections of the Mines, San Joaquin Republican (newspaper), January 24, 1852, Page 2.

48

California - with the exception of a balmy atmosphere and a rich soil."[73]

The emigrants, and dirty miners, had a tremendous need for bathing facilities; these needs were met in Stockton by May of 1850. "Public Baths for Stockton. We are much gratified to learn that Messrs, Annis and Latimer, Centre Street, have erected a new and elegant Bath House, and we are confident that all our fellow townsmen will participate most fully. In a town with a California climate, where the earth, by the continued action of the sun and travel, is separated into the most minute particles of dust, which is constantly in motion and adheres with great pertinacity to the surface of the body, nothing can be more conducive as a preventative of the health than the frequent ablutions of the person, either in cold or tepid water, according to the constitution of the individual. Let it suffice to say that one remedy, and one of the most effective, had been furnished by Annis and Latimer, hot and cold baths, which are worth all the 'pill-garlick stuff' in California."[74]

An immediate need in the gold fields was the need for law and order, and because of the coupling of the Mexican system of justice with the system brought from the East Coast by the argonauts, a new system of justice had to be developed in California that was understood and followed by both cultures. The cultural problems are well illustrated by one robbery reported in the San Joaquin Republican in 1851, "One of the most deliberate robberies we have ever heard of was committed on Wednesday last, at the forks of the road, where there are two sign posts; eight miles beyond the Stanislaus. As five persons, one named Mathew Rule, another Henry H. Tandy, two Frenchmen, and one Pole, on that day, were on their way to Stockton from the Mariposa mines, they were passed, between the Norweigian and Texas tents, by three Americans, two of whom rode splendid match horses, of a

---

[73]Ibid., Page 3.
[74]Stockton Times (newspaper), May 25, 1850.

strawberry roan color, and the other a brown mule. They saw them again at Burn's, again between the Tuolumne and Dry Creek, the robbers stopping at the Dry Creek tent until the travelers had passed, but overtook them at the forks of the road before described, and made the attack. One of the Frenchmen was in the wagon, and had a double barreled shot gun loaded with fine shot; but the robbers presented their pistols at him, and said, 'You d-drobber, we've got you now; get out of the wagon, and give up the money.' Mr. Rule, thinking that the Frenchman might have committed some robbery; told him to get out; the poor fellow got out accordingly. The scoundrels then attacked Rule, demanded his money, said it was their business to rob, and intended to have all the party was worth. Each of them had two six-shooters and long knives. Rule and his companions had no arms, and, therefore, were compelled to yield up their purses, amounting to $214. They then drove their victims into a hollow, bound them, and after unhitching their teams, tied them up to the wagons, administered a draught of water to each of the captives, and coolly left them."[75]

Even in the towns crime became a problem; San Francisco was not exempt from the greed of the lazy and desperate. On February 19, 1851, the store of Jansen, Bond, & Company, on Montgomery Street was robbed of two thousand dollars in gold coin. The Alta California editorialized against the state of crime, "One of the most bare-faced, cool, and audacious robberies of which annals of any country give a history, was perpetrated last evening. About eight o'clock, Mr. Charles J. Jansen was in his store, on Montgomery Street, two doors for Washington, when to men entered and wished to be shown some blankets. Mr. Jansen, who was, when they entered, in a partially reclining position on his counter, rose to serve them, when one of them drew from his pocket a slung-shot, with which he struck Mr. Jansen three times over the right temple, knocking him senseless on the floor. When

---

[75]San Joaquin Republican (newspaper), June 28, 1851.

Mr. Jansen recovered his senses he found that his desk, containing about two thousand dollars, had been opened and the money taken. Mr. Jansen's wound, which was immediately dressed by Dr. Temple, is not considered dangerous, as the skull is not fractured, although it is a wonder that he was not killed.

Thus, almost in broad daylight, the store of a peaceable citizen is entered, and a robbery, and almost a murder committed. In such a state of things, who is safe? Is there no remedy? No means by which the perpetrators of these outrages may be ferreted out and brought to justice? If once caught, if the law cannot punish them, an indignant community will."[76]

The robber was apprehended the next day by the San Francisco police. He was James Stuart, a member of the Sydney Ducks, a notorious group of renegades from Australia, who would rather rob than work for their livelihood.

Justice was sometimes lacking in the new society. To protect their mining rights, that is their greed, the assembly passed a mining tax to attempt to force foreign miners off their claims. The Stockton Times of May 11, 1850 provided a copy of the bill on page one. "An Act for the better regulation of the mines and the government of foreign miners. The People of the State of California, represented in Senate and Assembly, do enact as follows:

#1. No person who is not a native or naturalized citizen of the United States, or who may not have become a citizen under the teaty of Guadalupe Hidalgo (All native California Indians excepted), shall be permitted to mine in any part of this state without having first obtained a license so to do according to the provision of this act.

---

[76]Alta California (newspaper), February 20, 1851, Page 2.

#2. The governor shall appoint a collector of licenses to foreign miners for each of the mining counties, and for the county of San Francisco, who, before entering upon the duties of his office, shall take the oath required by the constitution, and shall give bond to the state with at least two good and sufficient sureties conditioned for the faithful performance of his official duties, which bond shall be approved by the governor and filed in the office of the secretary of state.

#6. Every person required by the first section of this act to obtain a license to mine, shall apply to the collector of licenses to foreign miners, and take out a license to mine, for which he shall pay the sum of twenty dollars per month.

#8. Should any foreigner or foreigners, after having been stopped by a Sheriff or Deputy Sheriff from mining in one place, seek a new location and continue such mining operations, it shall be deemed a misdemeanor, for which such offender, or offenders shall be arrested as for a misdemeanor, and he or they shall be imprisoned for a term not exceeding three months, and fined not more than a thousand dollars.

#9. It shall be the duty of the Secretary of State, immediately after the passage of this Act, to have two thousand copies each, in English and Spanish, printed and sent to the mining districts for circulation among the miners, and also to have the same published for thirty days in the Pacific News at San Francisco, and in some newspaper at Sacramento City and at Stockton.[77]

These regulations, and the others, of the 15 articles, illustrate the prejudice, inequality, and lack of justice in mining laws in the gold fields.

The hardworking population had an unfulfilled need for alcoholic beverages; these needs were soon filled. Finley, Johnson & Co. on Clay Street in San Francisco saw the need and were soon advertising, "Fresh flour, sherry wines in barrels and cases; maraschino, mosto, claret, cecilia and priorato

---

[77]Stockton Times (newspaper), May 11, 1850, Page 2.

wines, cognac, super cordials, gin, segars, leaf and chewing tobacco, and many other desirable articles."[78]

With a limited supply and great demand for most articles, the prices were unheard of in the east. "For the last three pair of boots I have had, I have paid, respectively, $18, $14, and $12 per pair. Other things are at corresponding prices in this place but at the mines every thing is much higher. Flour and pork vary in the mines from $40 to $200 per barrel. Common shoes, worth in Boston about 75 cents per pair, sell at $8, or even $12 per pair. There is a kind of recklessness about these prices which would be sought after in vain in any other part of the world. I saw a box of Seidlitz powders, worth 50 cents in San Francisco, sold in the mines for $24 in grain gold; and was credibly informed that brandy had been sold at $48 per bottle."[79]

Transportation to the mines from the cities, was crucial to the rapidly growing society. Two main sources of commercial transportation were the stagecoaches and ships. "The California State Company controlled all of the northern routes and Dooley & Co. and Fisher and Co. the southern routes. The pioneer line of the state ran from Sacramento to Mormon Island in September, 1849. The fare was $16, distance fourteen miles. In April, 1850 a stage line was established between San Francisco and San Jose, fare $32. Stockton and Sacramento were then, as they are now, the terminal water points."[80]

Boat transportation was also established early. Fares would fluctuate markedly; some boat trips were successful, but others ended in disaster; the Stockton Times reported on November 2, 1850: "Steamship Sagamore blown up, and

---

[78]Alta California (newspaper), May 31, 1849, Page 2.
[79]Ibid., Page 4.
[80]Geore H. Tinkham, California Men and Events, 1915, Page 115.

about fifty lives lost. About six o'clock yesterday afternoon, our citizens were stricken with terror and grief at the report of the terrible explosion of the boilers of the steamer Sagamore. She was leaving her berth on Central Wharf, bound for Stockton, and full of passengers, when her boilers burst with a tremendous explosion, and she instantly became a perfect wreck. It is impossible to conceive a more perfect mess of finely splintered ruins than she presented at the time of our visit. The loss of life must have been frightful. Fragments of mangled human remains were seen by spectators thrown high into the air and scattered around over the surrounding waters. We learn that she had a large number of passengers on board, among whom were several females. It is estimated that there were over one hundred souls on board, and of these scarcely more than one quarter escaped. Some few were picked up alive from the water, many of whom were badly injured, and a few crawled out from the fragments of the wreck and were landed on the wharf. A large number of the dead were taken to the hospital and to private quarters. The office of her owners, G.M. Burnham and Captain Griffin at Whitehall, was thronged with those who were anxious to obtain particulars. The deepest sorrow was visible on every countenance. Captain Griffin's loss is covered by insurance. We learn that there are in the city hospital, from the Sagamore-

Franco, French or Spanish
Stephen Smallfield, fireman
Eneso Poraca, Spanish
Leonard Hinckley and William Hathaway
James Lloyd, cook of the boat

One man, dead drunk, was thrown between 20 and 30 feet into the air, fell in the water, not seriously injured. A spectator states that he saw two barrels filled with the fragments of bodies, heads, arms, legs, viscera. One man, of whom we learn, was extremely fortunate. He had taken passage on Monday in the Maraposa, and returned from her wreck yesterday. Curious to say, he escaped again in this dire calamity."[81]

After all the hard work, and hardships overcome, Sundays were a welcome change. "The morals of the miners should be noticed. No man worked on Sunday at digging for gold; but that day was spent in prospecting in the neighborhood by the more sedate portion of the miners; while others spent it in playing at poker, with lumps of gold for checks [may be chocks; microfilm unreadable]; others collected in groups, might be seen under the shades of neighboring trees, singing songs, playing at old sledge and drinking whiskey; in all of which proceedings harmony, fun and good will to each other was the predominate feature. We had ministers of the gospel amongst us, but they never preached. Religion has been forgotten, even by its ministers, and instead of pointing out the narrow paths that led to eternal happiness to the diggers, there they might have been seen with pick-axe and pan traveling on trodden ways in search of filthy lucre and treasures that fadeth away or drinking good health and prosperity with friends."[82] Adolphus Windeler, an early prospector, wrote about the need to get caught up after a week of digging, " Sunday I washed and mended and done different things. Fixed our broken pick and made a shovel handle."[83]

A release, after the draining physical work of prospecting, digging, building coffer and wing dams, attempting to divert entire streams, and providing for their own existence, was needed. The miners were in a mood for fun.

---

[81]Stockton Times (newspaper), November 2, 1850, Page 1.
[82]San Joaquin Republican (newspaper), January 17, 1852, page 3.
[83]Adolphus Windeler, The California Gold Rush Diary of a German Sailor, Edited by W. Turrentine Jackson. 1969, Page 73.

NEED FOR FUN

Because of the tremendous stresses put on the gold-seekers caused by loneliness for women, homesickness, extremely hard physical labor, thirst, poor medical care, if any, and a poor diet, the miner was in the mood for fun and entertainment after he left his claim. This was especially true in the winter season when many left their gold-producing gravels and went to Benicia, Sacramento, Stockton, or even back to San Francisco.

One of the most accessible forms of entertainment was gambling. "Public gambling flourished as a legally authorized vice at all saloons, yet its prevalence led in the cities to the establishment of special gambling-houses. Mining, being itself a chance occupation, gave here an additional impulse to the passtime, which some cultivated as a mental stimulant, others as an anesthetic. With easy acquisition losses were less poignant. In San Francisco the plaza was the centre of these resorts, with the El Dorado saloon as the dividing point between the low places to the north and the select clubs southward. [Other gambling establishments were the Rendezvous, Bella Union, Verandah, Parker House, Aguila de Oro, and the Empire.] These and other attractions are employed to excite the senses, and breakdown all barriers before the strongest temptation, the piles of silver and gold in coin, dust and glittering lumps which border the leather-covered gaming-tables. The chief games were faro, preferred by Americans and Britons; monte, beloved of the Latin race, roulette, rouge-et-noir, rondo, vingt-et-un, paire-ou-non, trente-et-quarante, and chuck-a-luck with dice. The stakes ranged usually between fifty cents and five dollars, but rose frequently to $500 and $1,000 while amounts as high as $45,000 are spoken of as being risked upon the turn of a card. The most reckless patrons were richly laden miners, who instead of pursuing their intended journey homeward, surrendered here their hard-earned wealth, and returned sadder, if not wiser, to fresh toil and hardship."[84]

"The gambling saloons of 1848 and 1849 were large tents with dirt floors, and the tables usually were several planks laid across two sawhorses. The men sat on empty barrels or shipping crates more often than on chairs. Everyone gambled in 1849 and 1850, from the day laborer to the judges and merchants. Of the few hundred women in San Francisco, only a handful were 'ladies'. These women felt free to frequent the same saloons and gambling rooms as their male clientele. 'Abandoned women visit these places openly', observed one 49'er. 'I saw one the other evening sitting quietly at the monte-table, dressed in white pants, blue coat, and cloth cap, curls dangling over her cheeks, cigar in her mouth and a glass of punch at her side. She handled a pile of doubloons with her blue kid-gloved hands, and bet mostly boldly.

Most gamblers, however, were honest men. The professionals who rented a permanent place at a table usually left their winnings behind unguarded when they got up to take a break. San Francisco was a violent and vice-ridden town in 1849, but money was exposed in such a way as would be thought madness in any other part of the world according to J.D. Borthwick. Maybe gold was so abundant that year and prices so high that money had lost its ordinary hold over men.

Men crowded the gambling saloons looking for more than the chance of winning money. Some enjoyed the excitement of watching others win and lose. Others were looking for friendly, comfortable surroundings in which to pass their free time."[85]

---

[84]Herbert Howe Bancroft, History of California, Volume VI, Pages 238-240.
[85]Charles Lockwood, Suddenly San Francisco: The Early Years of an Instant City, San Francisco Examiner special project, 1978, Pages 31-35.

"Drinking was the only pastime that rivaled prostitution and gambling. In 1849 and 1850 bars were usually part of a gambling establishment. Most men did not know what to make of openly flourishing prostitution, gambling and drinking when they arrived in San Francisco."[86]

Losses were the order of the day. "One day a Mexican rode up to a gambling saloon at Mission Dolores. Dismounting, he tied his horse, entered, and began betting. Soon his money, pistols, and all his belongings were gone. Finally his horse was staked and lost; but this was more than he could endure, and he determined to save it. As he rose from the table he managed to upset it, and while all were engaged in picking up the scattered money, he slipped out, mounted, and galloped away."[87]

"There was a beautiful little French woman who kept a roulette table at the north end of Montgomery Street. There were many such in San Francisco. The room was elegantly furnished like a boudoir. The syren sat behind the table, elegantly arrayed in black silk, her face fronting the open door, whirling her wheel most bewitchingly. Before her lay a pile of silver dollars and gold ounces. A tall bony New Englander, brought up on mush, catechism, and Poor Richard's almanac, passing by, stopped to survey the scene. He caught the infection. Throwing looks at languishing lips and voluptuous form, he entered and seated himself before her. First he lay down gold pieces, then silver, all the time almost invariably losing. Then he brought out a watch, then another watch, and another. He had had a luck game of poker the night before which accounted for the watches. The charmer swept them all to her side of the table."[88]

---

[86] Ibid., Page 36.
[87] Herbert Howe Bancroft, Bancroft's Works, Volume XXXV, 1846-1856, Page 718.
[88] Ibid., Page 716.

Sometimes the gambling was totally reckless. "It was a common practice for miners to lay an unopened bag of dust upon a card, call the amount of his venture, and if he won receive the same from the dealer without opening his bag at all. One night, a Mexican with his face half concealed in an old serape, entered the El Dorado, and edging his way through the crowd stepped before a monte table. After following the game for a short time, he drew forth an old linen bag of coin, supposed of course to be silver dollars, and placing it upon a card leaned over the table, and forsaken by his usual stoicism, watched the dealer's fingers with breathless anxiety. The Mexican won; the dealer with quiet indifference pulled the bag over to him, untied the string, and emptied out the contents. His face turned white as a sheet, even his customary coolness deserted him; for out of the bag had rolled, not silver dollars as everyone supposed, but golden doubloons, more than enough to break the bank."[89] This was entertainment in 1850.

"There was great rivalry among the gambling houses as to which could offer its customers the best entertainment. El Dorado retained its wheezy old orchestrion to the end of its days, but also employed as many gifted soloists as could be procured. The Verandah presented a marvel who might well be called the daddy of the modern jazz trap-drummer. When equipped for a musical evening, he wore pipes tied to his chin, a drum strapped to his back, drumsticks fastened to his elbows, and cymbals attached to his wrists. All of these instruments he played more or less in unison at approximately the same time. Moreover, he patted his feet, which were encased in enormous hard-soled shoes, and with them made a tremendous clatter upon the floor. In several establishments women played harps and pianos, and each evening at the Alhambra a French-woman performed upon the violin, for which she received daily two ounces of gold dust, or about thirty-two dollars. The Aguila de Oro had a Negro chorus

---

[89]Ibid., Page 718.

during the autumn of 1849, which introduced spirituals into California; and the Bella Union offered a Mexican quintet, consisting of two harps, two guitars, and a flute."[90]

---

[90]The Palace Hotel, The Barbary Coast: The Miners Came in Forty-Nine, Page 25.

Norris, Gregg, & Norris $5.00

Norris, Gregg, & Norris $5.00

Hiram Norris' Property 2001

Looking West from Hiram Norris' Lot

Stockton Channel 1850
Courtesy of San Joaquin County Museum

Adobe Ruins in Benicia 2001

Grave of Charles Gregg

Graves of Thomas & Hiram Norris

Grave of Thomas Norris

Grave of Hiram Norris

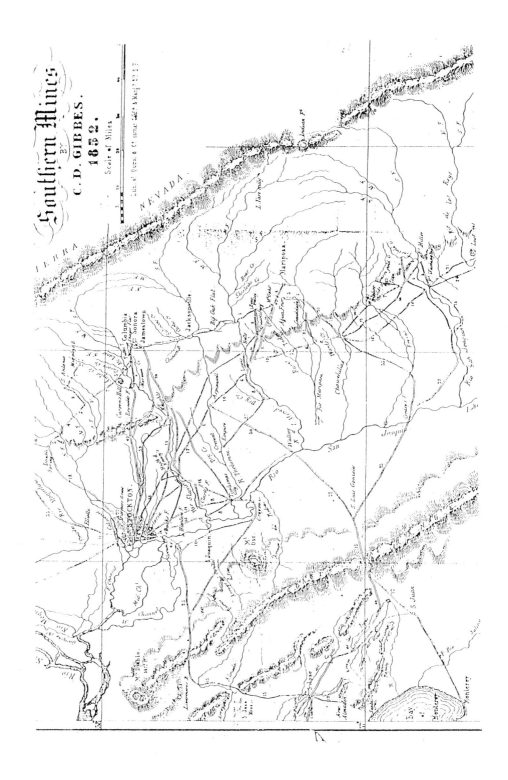

Southern Mines.

BY

C. D. GIBBES.

1852.

Scale of Miles

After the return of the Lewis and Clark Expedition, the major effort at commerce was carried on by the fur traders; British, Canadian, and American. In the Northwest, where the majority of trading was done by barter, the first coins to appear were brought west by the Hudson's Bay Company and the North West Company.

The North West Company brought a few copper tokens to trade for furs with the Indians; the various Indian tribes did not understand the value of the coins and used them for jewelry, or decorations. Most of these copper, or bronze, coins were holed in order to be hung on buckskin laces. These tokens were dated 1820, long before the gold rush of 1849 in California. The Hudson Bay Company used trade goods, and especially blankets, to trade for furs with the Indians and white trappers. Five beaver pelts would be sufficient to buy one Hudson Bay blanket.

In the 1830's, the first American missionaries arrived in the Willamette Valley of Oregon and could only buy supplies from Hudson's Bay trading posts. Dudley McClure, in his book on the Oregon Beaver coins, writes, "cash from those who had it was gladly accepted, but such coins went out on the next ship to the home office in London."[91]

The next western migration was of the American settlers who crossed America in 1845, 1846, and 1847. McClure summed up the coinage situation, "Only a few, at best, had even small amounts of cash to tide them over until they could build shelters and find acreage to clear and plant crops upon. Fortunate were those who drove cattle, sheep and horses

---

[91]Dudley L. McClure, Tales of the Golden Beavers, Publishing Co. & date unknown, Page 6.

across the long trail. The animals rated high in trade. Difficulties of frontier trade without money, were explained by Peter H. Burnett, an Oregon Pioneer who went to the gold-rush and stayed on to become California's first governor, "for example, a farmer may have a pair of oxen for sale, and may want a pair of plow-horses. In case there be no circulating medium, he will have great difficulty in making an exchange."[92]

Because of the problems transacting business that existed, in sessions of the Oregon Legislature, the delegates approved a long list of commodities as legal tender: butter, wheat, hides, tallow, lard, beef, pork, peas, lumber and other export items. However, Governor Abernethy did not sign the bill. The next bill, which did pass, included gold, silver, wheat, treasury drafts, and approved orders on solvent merchants as legal tender. Abernethy, who owned a store in Oregon City, went one step further; he issued rock money made out of "small pieces of flint bearing paper slips with his name and a value good for exchange at his store."[93]

"Under the conditions that existed, it can be seen that the American store-keepers were at a disadvantage. While the law named certain items as legal tender, the accepted basic exchange unit continued to be the beaver pelt as backed by the Hudson's Bay Company through its well-stocked trading posts. It was under this cumbersome arrangement, a mostly barter-and trade economy, that the Oregon Country was operating when the flood of California gold was superimposed upon it. One of the earliest gold trickles was the dust brought in on the brig 'Sabine' from the Golden Gate pueblo of San Francisco in December, 1848."[94]

"Some 6,000 to 8,000 of the Oregon Argonauts, it was estimated, took the wilderness trails south - 600 to 900 miles,

---

[92]Ibid., Page 7.
[93]Ibid., Page 8.
[94]Ibid., Page 8.

depending on the starting point - after word of the unbelievable gold discovery reached them in late July of 1848. Many were home again in four to six months, their individual 'takes' ranging generally from $1,000 to $2,000 and up into the $30,000 - $40,000 category. By early March of 1849, at least $2,000,000 in gold dust had been brought home by the first wave of returning miners. More was yet to come. And, the rest of the world was just starting to the big gold rush of 1849."[95]

"Out of necessity the raw gold had been forced into use as money, and that was the root of the foul-up. It became the West Coast's main medium of exchange, substituting for coins which were all but non-existent. As such, the precious dust was hard to handle and subject to debasement."[96]

"At best, the nuggets and dust, hoarded in the universally carried accouterment, the leather poke, were inconvenient to handle in small transactions. However, the pinch amounts varied with the size of people's thumbs. There were marked variances, too, in the weighing of larger gold amounts as tallied on the frontier's conglomeration of scales and what passed as scales."[97] "Added to these inconsistencies were the variations in content of the native gold, some almost pure and some naturally alloyed heavily with silver. Besides the dust's lack of uniformity, there was considerable loss in handling."[98]

The tremendous wealth that existed, in both the ground and in the miners' bags, made the society careless with the gold that they had earned. Besides the carelessness, the lack of coinage made the use of gold dust and small nuggets imperative. Just how careless is well illustrated by George H. Bernhard, whose father was an early miner in Mariposa in

---

[95]Ibid., Page 5.
[96]Ibid., Page 5.
[97]Ibid., Page 9.
[98]Ibid., Page 9.

1849. "Most of the goods bought by the miners were paid for with gold dust. Small purchases were paid for with a pinch of gold from a buckskin bag or poke. In the larger transactions, the gold was weighed and was worth from $14 to $18 an ounce, according to purity. Saturday night was always the big night and quite a lot of gold was spilled on the floor. On Sunday morning, you could always find old Balty and his squaw, with their pan, brush and basket. They would sweep the full length of the store, put the dirt in their basket, take it down to the creek and pan it. They made pretty good wages with the sweepings."[99]

In response to all the various problems mentioned, the Oregon citizens of the new territory took the matter into their own hands. Eight leaders of the area created the Oregon Exchange Company and started a private mint in Oregon City, Oregon Territory. It was this group of eight that produced the $5.00 and $10.00 golden Beavers; they were coined in an old house above the falls.

---

[99]Newell D. Chamerlain, The Call of Gold: True Tales on the Gold Road to Yosemite, Valley Publishers, 1977, Pages 101-102.

The rolling hills of Contra Costa County, in the Bay Area of northern California provided a beautiful setting for a small community. The fantastic climate and lovely shores of the Carquinez Straits added to the beauty of the location. Below these hills, the early California pioneers selected a spot to develop the town-site of Benicia. In 1847, land speculators dreamed of a big city; little realizing the tremendous wealth that was waiting to be unearthed further east. The town had first been called Francesca and later changed to Benicia, in honor of General Vallejo's wife, Francesca Benicia Felipsa Carrillo.

The early speculators believed that their new community, instead of San Francisco, would become the metropolis of the western shores. Robert Semple and T.O. Larkin were busy promoting the town-site. Dr. Semple, who lived in Benicia, wrote Larkin, still living in San Francisco, on July 12, 1847, "The plan for the city is now finished...a number of lots have been selected by men who will build on them. It is pretty well ascertained that there is a great abundance of coal at a point opposite Mare Island. We need lumber; if I had 50,000 feet I could sell it for cash in three weeks. Come up and spend a week at the place, come by land and you will have no trouble in crossing, we crossed 24 horses on Sunday last and had no trouble. I am having some deeds printed with my own name."[100] Thus, already the ferry was started by Semple; by September he had the canal done and work had started on a wharf.

"In either August or September, 1847, Capt. E.H. Von Phfister, a native of New York City, who had been in the habit of trading on this coast, arrived from Honolulu, bringing with

---

[100]Jacqueline McCart Woodruff, The Promise of California, University of California Master's Thesis, 1947, Page 17.

him a stock of goods, which he opened and displayed in the adobe store. This being 25 X 40 was commodious enough to accommodate everybody in want of lodgings by night. The Captain being one of the jovial and hospitable sort, everybody was at home in his presence or under his roof."[101]

"It was in April, 1848 that the men of Benicia, who usually congregated at Von Pfister's store, were gathered there discussing the future of the country under the new ownership, for the treaty of Guadalupe Hidalgo had been signed two months previous and the country had become a part of the United States. Coal mines were then considered the big things, and the men speculated on the good fortune which would come to them should one be discovered in the vicinity. A stranger, by the name of Charles Bennett, spoke up and said that something better than a coal mine had been discovered where he was working. Bennett had been engaged with James Marshall at Coloma in building a mill for General Sutter, and was then on his way to Monterey, taking with him some specimens of gold to have them tested, as there was no acid for this purpose available at any nearer point. He displayed to the little group of Benicians about four ounces in small pieces such as had first been discovered when the water was turned on to run [deepen the millrace] the mill. A profound impression was made on the little group by the sight of the yellow metal."[102] Bennett had come down the Siskiyou Trail to California from Oregon. He is quoted as saying, "Coal! I've got something here which will beat coal and make this the greatest country in the world."[103] There is evidence that Sutter wanted the military governor, General Richard B. Mason, to approve a lease of 10-12 square miles around the mill; this

---

[101]Wood, Alley & Company, History of Solano County, 1879, Page 151.
[102]Marguerite Hunt, History of Solano County, Volume 1, 1926, Page 192.
[103]Richard Dillion, Great Expectations - The Story of Benicia, California, 1980, Pages 32-33.

was outside the original Mexican land grant. "Governor Mason turned Sutter down on March 5. With regret, he informed Sutter he could not sanction the contract because the government did not recognize the right of Indians to sell or lease the lands they occupied. The secret was out, thanks to Bennett's bragging. It was soon confirmed when three Mormon workmen of Sutter's, enroute home to Salt Lake City, also stopped in Benicia. They showed the bug-eyed Benicians more gold and assured them that there was plenty for all around Sutter's Mill. The Gold Rush began in Benicia."[104]

The hopes and dreams of a great city were temporarily wrecked when the gold was discovered at Sutter's mill. The quick reversal of fortunes was amply illustrated in a letter that John Bidwell wrote from new Helvetia on May 15, 1848, "I wish to sell two leagues of land adjoining Larkin's Children's Rancho the place is worth $1,000. I will trade it for live stock if you want it. The gold excitement is making lands up here more valuable - the gold has been found for more than forty miles. There is much exaggeration - the facts are a man will average about $10 per day." Soon after, Sam Brannan, editor of the California Star, on his way to Coloma, persuaded Captain Von Pfister, an old shipmate, to pack his goods into Semple's ferry boat and to open a store at the mines. Before leaving Benicia, Von Pfister wrote to Larkin: "The town is almost deserted as the gold fever is raging to a tremendous extent in this part of the county. For the past two months business has been at a standstill in Benicia, and I feel I must leave if I am to survive. He promised Larkin that if he were fortunate, the whole of it would go to improve Benicia."[105]

How ironic that the town was settled for coal, while gold was so near. Soon, however, Benicia became the gateway to the mines. "On the same date Semple wrote to Larkin that he

---

[104]Ibid., Page 33.
[105]Jacqueline McCart Woodruff, The Promise of California, University of California Master's Thesis, 1947, Page 26.

did not blame Von Pfister for leaving, for he had a good offer, but that his own situation was bad.

"In no more than three days there will probably not be more than two men here; all have gone to the gold mines. I have not been able to get but two men to stay with me. I have laid up the Green Horne and will probably run the ferry boat alone. They are offering from three to five dollars per day for men, a price which I cannot afford to pay."

"Semple's boat was chartered to take Von Pfister's goods to the mines for what was termed a "fantastic sum" and in six days Von Pfister reached Coloma with his goods. Dr. Semple, on returning from his chartered trip to the mines, found some thirty men waiting for passage across the straits. Brannan and Von Pfister did a thriving business until October when Von Pfister sold out and left the mines to return to Benicia. In the spring of 1849, Von Pfister rented an adobe and operated a hotel at considerable profit. Gold seekers came up from San Francisco and many times laid over at Benicia while waiting for a steamer or stage coach for Sacramento."[106] VonPfister later sold his interest in the firm when his brother from Honolulu joined him at Benicia. The brother was murdered; Von Pfister traveled for a year trying to locate the killer, was unsuccessful, and returned to Benicia where he was in business, and lived there the rest of his life. The adobe ruins of Von Pfister's store still exist on D Street. His private residence, for which he bought the lot in 1849 for $3,000, still exists, in 2001, in beautiful condition; it is located at 280 West J. Street.

"During the winters of 1849 and 1850, large numbers of miners returned to Benicia. There were those who returned to spend their gold in the usual riot and others who returned to try their luck in safer pursuits. During this period, Von Pfister paid five hundred dollars a month rent, one hundred and fifty dollars for a cook, one hundred and a quarter dollars each for two

----

[106]Ibid., Page 33.

stewards, one hundred dollars each for a housekeeper and bartender. Notwithstanding this heavy expense, Von Pfister cleared $12,000 in eleven months. At this time he sold a lot on the corner of Pine and Dupont streets in San Francisco for $2,500 and immediately invested it in Benicia property. Stores and dwellings were soon built as the town prospered."[107] "Saloons and gambling halls - critics termed them 'gambling hells' - were soon in full blast. Von Pfister's rude saloon was eclipsed by the likes of Tom McGuire's gin mill adjacent to the presitigious Solano Hotel on the corner of First and E Streets. The finest establishment in the state, it boasted two bars and a band of noble musicians. A rival of the Solano, of course, was Major Cooper's California House on West H Street."[108]

"The dreams were temporarily crushed when inflowing fleets of the world dropped anchor and unloaded passengers and freight at the revival city, San Francisco. In 1849, however, Commodore Thomas Ap Catesby Jones brought his fleet up to the harbor at Benicia, and a military post and supply depot were established nearby. Further encouragement was given the next year when the Pacific Mail Steamship Company chose Benicia as the site of its shops and depot, a choice which brought wharf improvements, additional capital, and demands for labor and produce. In 1850, the population numbered about 1,000. Benicia was incorporated as a city and became the county seat of Solano County."[109]

In the April 19, 1849, issue of Alta California, E. Mickle & Co. announced, "that they were now unloading the barque Tasso and the brig Progresso, just arrived from Valparaiso. To accommodate purchasers from the interior, the most extensive arrangements have been made for the conveyance of goods from Benicia to Sacramento City, Stockton, and other points, at

---

[107]Ibid., Page 26.
[108]Gold Rush, Oregon Historical Quarterly, Volume 1, Pages 44-45.
[109]California Historical Society Quarterly, Volume 17, September 1938, Pages 261-163.

one half the rate of freights now charged from San Francisco on goods destined for the same places."[110]

"Mrs. Martha Fisher Quinn, a lifelong resident of Benicia, recalls hearing her mother tell of the days of splendor following the gold rush. She is the daughter of Joseph Fisher, who came to Benicia in 1849, and opened a market there, and the niece of Captain Von Pfister, the third settler. Her aunt, Mrs. Sheridan, was a belle of San Francisco, but moved to Benicia in the '50's and her wedding to Captain Von Pfister was marked by a week's open house and such entertaining as was the marvel of the town. Many a time, she declares, she has heard of her uncle having traded his merchandise for a bottle of gold dust."[111]

As businesses were established and commerce grew rapidly, it wasn't long before some enterprising businessmen in Benicia made a huge splash in the San Francisco newspapers. In terms of numismatic history, of the United States, an even bigger splash was made. The May 31, 1849 issue of the Alta California newspaper wrote the following:

> Gold coining. We have in our possession, a five
> dollar gold coin, struck at Benicia City, though the imprint
> is San Francisco. In its general appearance, it resembles
> the United States coin of the same value, but it bears
> the private stamp of "Norris, Greig, & Norris," and is in
> other particulars widely different.
> We learn also, that Mr. Theodore Dubosq, a jeweller from
> Philadelphia, who recently arrived in the Grey Eagle,
> has brought with him the necessary machinery for
> striking private coin.[112]

---

[110]Alta California (newspaper), April 19, 1849, Page 1.
[111]Marguerite Hunt, History of Solano County, Volume 1, 1926, Page 203.
[112]Alta California (newspaper), May 31, 1849, Page 1.

A mystery had been created. Where, in Benicia, were the coins produced? Who made them? Where did the coiners go after leaving Benicia? Mr. Donald H. Kagin in his fantastic book, Private Gold Coins and Patterns of the United States, writes, "It has never been determined where in Benicia the first Norris, Gregg & Norris coins were minted. The late San Francisco historian, Roy Hill, published an article by L.P. Marshall, written for the February 1912 issue of Out West. In it the author states that while he was roaming the region around Benicia with his sons in 1852-1853, he was told of an old house which he proceeded to occupy. Marshall continues, 'In and about the house we found appliances for the manufacture of counterfeit coins, such as crucibles, dies, copper, etc. It is supposed that a band of counterfeiters had found the place deserted and had taken possession of it.' If Marshall is correct in his assumption, however, then why would the coiners abandon their eqipment, without any apparent justification?

It is possible that this house was indeed occupied by counterfeiters, although according to Eckfeldt and DuBois, no counterfeits were ever found (i.e., known to them in the 1850's) from among the California gold coins. The home could also have been a proposed site of the Mormons, who at one time had planned to settle there. This, however, is highly unlikely because no mention is made in the Mormon journals of a proposed mint in California. It is possible that Marshall may have used the word 'counterfeiter' for anyone other than the government who made coins. Until positive evidence to the contrary is forthcoming, the house Marshall discovered may be assumed to be the site of the Norris, Gregg, & Norris mint."[113]

Two years later, on October 15, 1851, the San Joaquin Republican carried a story which had been printed in the Alta California paper, that a discovery of gold had been made at Benicia. "Between forty and fifty dollars were said to have

---

[113]Donald H. Kagin, Private Gold Coins & Patterns of the United States, 1981, Page 64.

been taken out yesterday, and quite a number had gone to the new placer to stake out their claims."[114]

As late as the 1860's, Benicia was still in the news of the West Coast. "The Army's Department of the Pacific, under the command of General John E. Wood, was supplying army outposts in Oregon with muskets, ammunition, and military supplies."[115] These were being shipped to Fort Dalles, Fort Orford, and Fort Lane, eight miles from Jacksonville, where rich deposits of gold were being discovered. Ironically, gold was also discovered south of Ft. Dalles and at Gold Beach near Fort Orford.

---

[114]San Joaquin Republic (newspaper), October 15, 1851, Page 1.
[115]Conditions of the Fifties, Oregon Historical Quarterly, Volume 8, Page 194.

STOCKTON AND THE SOUTHERN MINES

"San Francisco", "Sutter", "James Marshall", "Placerville"; these words have evoke memories of the famous California gold rush of '49. In the common lore of the western history of the United States much less is generally known and written about the Southern mines. It was to this area that many of the early prospectors, and territorial coiners, moved from San Francisco, Benicia, and many of the other mining districts.

Once the cry of "gold" was heard, it wasn't long before the sailing ships and the steamers were landing their passengers at San Francisco. From there, they would take river boats up the San Joaquin River to Stockton, which was the terminus of water travel. They then would walk, ride, or take the stagecoaches to the Southern Mines.

"Stockton was founded in 1849 by Captain Charles M. Weber. When first he saw the land he believed in some future time it would become a city of great commercial importance because of its deep water outlet to the sea. Previously, the land was designated by the Mexicans as Campo de Los Franceses, the camp of the Frenchmen. A man named William Gulnac, being a naturalized Mexican citizen, obtained the grant free of cost."[116]

Before the discovery of gold, the region around Stockton had been populated by the Miwok tribe; the local branch near Stockton was known as the Si-yak-um-na. Estimates of the Indian population, before the white man came, are unknown. "When Colonel J.J. Warner visited the San Joaquin and Sacramento valleys in 1832 with the Ewing Young trapping expedition, he found a more numerous Indian population

------

[116]George Henry Tinkham, California Men and Events, Record Publishing Company, 1915, Page 72.

subsisting upon the natural products of the soil and waters than upon any other part of the continent where he had traveled. He explains that this heavy population was due to the plentiful supply of wild game, fish, nuts of the forest, and seeds. Indians did not cultivate the soil, but they were experts in catching fish, in many ways, and in snaring game. When he returned to the valleys in the late summer of 1833, Colonel Warner found that a great fever epidemic had practically depopulated the Indian residents. From the head of the Sacramento River to the great bend of the San Joaquin River, he saw only six or eight live Indians, but the party found large numbers of skulls and dead bodies near the now deserted rancherias as well as many graves and remains of funeral pyres. By 1852, when a census was taken of the Indians in San Joaquin County, there were only four rancherias left with a total population of about 390 Indians."[117]

One of the early settlers, a Mr. Callahan, was able to supply his needs by going out every morning to hunt elk among the tule; around daylight, the elk could be found in herds of forty or fifty. Survival was easy in this land of plenty; the environment would easily support this meager population.

There were several names before Stockton was chosen. Earlier it had been called Castoria in connection with French Camp, located a little south of present day Stockton; the word "castoria" meant beaver-settlement and was selected because of the large numbers of beavers trapped in the area by the southern brigades of the Hudson's Bay Company.

"Stockton" was a favorite name of Captain Weber because he had met Commodore Robert Field Stockton, commander of military forces in California, soon after he was a captive of the Mexican forces near Los Angeles. Years later, because the promises of Stockton never materialized, Weber

---

[117]Covert Martin, Stockton Album Through the Years, 1959, Page 15.

wished that he had retained the name Castoria for what was to become his city. The name San Joaquin was given to the valley of the rushes by Spanish explorer Gabriel Moraga in 1808. The first American to explore the area was Jedediah Smith, of the Rocky Mountain Fur Company, who passed through the area in late 1826 or early 1827. One of Smith's men, John Turner, led a trapping expedition of French-Canadian trappers to this area in 1828. The French parties returned to this area every year until 1846 and, in the process, missed the gold in the streams in which they trapped.

When gold was discovered at Sutter's Mill, Sutter decided to send some couriers to Monterey where chemicals were probably available to test the golden colored mineral samples. He swore the couriers to secrecy, but they stopped for the night at Tuleberg, told the few settlers about the discovery, and showed them samples of gold. The settlers waited for Captain Weber to return from the mountains and told him of the gold discovery; he was not surprised because earlier he had been given a little gold dust by the Indians when they traded at Weber's store in San Jose. Weber then took a party of men up the Stanislaus River, but without luck. They then moved to the Mokelumne River further north where they found gold; continuing north they found gold in every stream.

At one rich spot they made a semi-permanent camp and named the stream Weber's Creek. Captain Weber soon organized a joint stock company called the Stockton Mining Company. Weber outfitted the company from his little store and sent them back to the gold fields while he took a boat to San Francisco for additional supplies. Among the items he brought back were silver coins and trinkets to exchange for gold nuggets with the Indians. The members of this company were: John M. Murphy, Joseph Buzzell, Andrew Baker, Thomas Pyle, George Fraezer, and Dr. J.C. Isbel. Weber also recruited twenty-five Indians and sent them up to Weber's Creek to look for more gold. The Indians discovered some coarse gold higher up on the Stanislaus River.

"The gold found in California was of two kinds, scale gold and coarse gold. Of the latter many pieces are still in existence, in possession of those what took them from the ground. The gold was sent to San Francisco, where it was melted into bars. The dust was carried by the miners in a belt, made of material obtained from the Indians. It was made of strong buckskin, doubled, from two to four inches wide, with an opening at one end, and made so as to fasten around the body at the waist. By this means, the weight was distributed equally, and it is said that men have carried $15,000 in one of these belts."[118] When General Mason took his tour of the mines, he reported seeing 4,000 men digging for gold at Coloma, "and taking, per month, from the river bed, from $50,000 to $100,000. Their only tools were butcher knives, shovels and shallow pans. Two miners finding a 'pocket' of gold in Weber Creek cleared up to $17,000 in one week. The Indians working for John Sinclair brought in $19,000 in ten days."[119]

The amount of wealth that was coming out of the creeks was unimaginable. James H. Carson published a story in 1852 in "Early Recollections of the Mines" that illustrates the excitement of the times. "One day he saw a form, bent and filthy, approaching him. It was an old acquaintance whom Carson at first did not recognize, for his hair hung out of his hat, his chin with beard was black, and his buckskins reached to his knees; an old flannel shirt he wore, which many a bush had tore. This apparition had a great bag on its back. Then he told me that it was gold, and that he had made it in five weeks at Kelsey's and the dry diggings (where Placerville is now located). When Carson found this difficult to believe and asked to see the proof in the bag on his back, the man complied, and out the metal tumbled; not in dust or scales, but in pieces ranging in size from that of a pea to hen's eggs...and

---

[118]George Henry Tinkham, History of Stockton, 1880, Page 114.
[119]George Henry Tinkham, California Men & Events, 1915, Page 90.

then the fellow added, this is only what I picked out with a knife."[120] Carson was soon on his way to Weber's Creek.

Another early arrival in the Southern Mines was a Hispano-Californios, Antonio Franco Coronel, who joined the gold rush from Los Angeles. He was fascinated by the amount of gold that the Indians had accumulated. He secretly followed the Indians to a ravine known as Canada del Barro. "About a thousand yards long, it was very rich in gold. Coronel, on October 7, 1848, began to work a claim he had staked out and the first day recovered forty-five ounces of coarse gold. All of his companions had brilliant results, including one Lorenzo Soto who gathered approximately fifty-two pounds in about eight days."[121] The richest deposits were found in 1848, before the news reached the East Coast. In September 1848, in a dry ravine near the Stanislaus, a twenty-five pound piece of gold was found, and a twenty-seven ounce piece at Kelsey's Dry Diggings.

When Weber decided to prospect for gold himself, he requested his Indian friend, Jesus, to send him twenty-five laborers. This group of prospectors, working for Weber, were very lucky; by July of 1848 they discovered a huge nugget. "A very fine specimen of pure gold, weighing eighty and a half ounces avoirdupois, the general form of the nugget being that of a kidney. Its rare beauty, purity and size, caused the firm of Cross Hobson, of San Fancisco, to pay for it $3,000, being induced to pay this extraordinary price in order to secure so rare a nugget to send to the Bank of England as a specimen from the newly discovered gold fields of California. Gold dust was selling at that time for $12 per ounce, and the specimen, had it sold only for its value as metal, would have yielded the Stockton Mining Company only $966."[122]

---

[120]George Hammond, The Weber Era in Stockton History, 1982, Page 90.
[121]Ibid., Page 91.
[122]Lewis Publishing Company, An Illustrated History of San

77

The April 6, 1850, edition of the Stockton Times wrote of a Stockton citizen returning from the discoveries at Sonora. He reported, "There is no doubt that the new placer is of unprecedented richness, and there are supposed to be from three to five thousand persons at work upon it, who in numerous instances are getting from two to twenty ounces per day. Many of the holes have yielded each upwards of ten lbs. of the precious metal. From one hole a man took 37 pounds of gold in three days. This information may be relied upon as it comes from a highly respectable source."[123]

The Stockton Times newspaper in its April 13, 1850, edition wrote about a very rich strike, "...23 lbs. of gold in nine days. Two men lately took out from one hole in the Mormon Gulch 23 lbs. weight of gold in nine days. We have seen the gold, and are satisfied as to the accuracy of the statement."[124]

By May 11, 1850, the Stockton Times was writing that the mines are inexhaustible. A man arrived in Stockton and told the newspaper staff that a placer had been located in a site, which is now Columbia, in which the miners dug to a depth of sixty-two feet; they found gold four feet below the surface and the deposit continued down to the bottom of the hole. On the previous Friday, a miner found a lump of pure gold, weighing four pounds and seven ounces.

Because of all the rich strikes, the mines located further south began to assume real importance and subsequently drew the fortune-seekers by the hundreds. What was required was, "establishment of a place which could be relied upon as a general base of supplies. That base would naturally be the point where a combined summer and winter water navigation ceased in the approach to the mountains. This point was

---

Joaquin County, 1890, Page 62.
[123]Stockton Times (newspaper), April 13, 1850, Page 1.
[124]Ibid., April 6, 1850, Page 1.

where Weber had previously pitched his tent, at the head of the slough or channel which had already become known in the country as the place the Stockton Mining Co. had made the source of its supplies. Captain Weber, with his usual clear-headed manner of deducing the effect from an existing cause, decided that there was more money in founding a city than in digging for gold."[125]

E. Gould Buffum, who had been one of the first prospectors in 1848 and 1849, said about Weber, "The man who has been most fortunate in the mines is probably, Charles M. Weber...who before he gave up his life of miner and trader, had made between four and five hundred thousand dollars."[126] "When Charles' brother Adolph arrived in Stockton, he was amazed to learn of the wealth that Charles had acquired. Adolph and brokers in San Francisco warned Charles that the days of 1849-50 would not last, 'when the bottom of his cash box was lined with $60,000 to $80,000 worth of gold.' "[127] Later in 1855 appropriately Adolph tried to get a job in the U.S. Mint in San Francisco, but was unsuccessful. Soon Charles used his influence and Adolph was given a job as Deputy State Assayer in the Assayer's Office; he got the job in 1855.

By September 1848, he had given up mining and had gone into business. Chester S. Lyman, later a professor at Yale University, toured the California gold region, and noted in his diary on August 23 that Weber had "moved his [trading camp] to the diggings further south."[128] "As travelers these travelers must, out of necessity, have food and other supplies Captain Weber now concluded to establish a large commercial house. James Carson, after whom Carson's Hill is named, wrote of Weber's business in the foot hills: "So great was the

---

[125]San Joaquin Historical Society (Stockton newsletter).
[126]George Hammond, The Weber Era in Stockton History, 1982, Page 90.
[127]Ibid., Page 139.
[128]Ibid., Page 93.

income of the Captain's trading houses that he was daily sending out mules packed with gold to the settlements. His trading houses more likely were lean-to's or packhorses. Weber's brother Adolph, writing to their parents in 1853, claimed his brother had 'opened up 49 stores to provide the miners with all they needed.' One miner, R.F. Peckham, later reminisced, 'tools for mining purposes were scarce and high - a pick, pan, shovel ranging from $50 to $200; butcher's knives from $10 to $25, and cradle-washing machines from $200 to $800 each.'"[129] He planned to locate his store on the Peninsula, as the most suitable spot for a wholesale and retail house, but the mistake of the supercargo in misunderstanding Weber's orders caused Stockton to be founded on the block lying between Levee, Commerce, Main, and Center streets. Going to Yerba Buena, Weber chartered a vessel with instructions to sail to Santa Cruz and for a load of redwood lumber and transport it to Weber's embarcadero, the settlement being known by a half dozen different names. "The supercargo had been ordered, on arrival at Weberville, to unload the lumber on the north bank, but he unloaded on the south bank and Weber was compelled to erect his store where the lumber was because of a scarcity of laborers, and no bridges nor boats to move it across."[130]

Earlier, Charles Weber had gone into business partnership with William Gulnac, a Mexican citizen, in San Jose; they had a store, flour mill, bakery, salt works and a blacksmith shop. In 1843 Gulnac applied to governor Manuel Micheltorena for a land grant around the Hudson's Bay trapper's area, which later became Frenchtown. "In January, 1844, the grant was approved for eleven square leagues, or 48,747 acres and was called El Rancho del Campo de los

---

[129]George Henry Tinkham, History of San Joaquin County, 1923, Page 53.
[130]Covert Martin, Stockton Album Through the Years, 1959, Page 18.

80

Franceses grant."[131] Once again Weber was in the right place at the right time when Gulnac sold him his interest in the property for $50.00 of groceries and a white horse. Historians have valued the entire deal at about sixty dollars.

Weber's next goal was to attract settlers to the area. By 1846 he had attracted about twenty settlers who had been trappers and sailors. When the war trouble with Mexico broke out, they left to move near military protection on the coast. In 1847, Weber offered a block of land in Stockton and a Spanish section of 480 acres outside of Stockton to each settler. "Settlers began to accept the offers. One of them was Joseph Buzzell who owned Block 1 and a 160-acre ranch along the Calaveras. He erected the first wooden building of oak logs in Stockton, in 1847, at Center Street and Weber Avenue."[132] Weber, to serve the new arrivals, established a small store, also at the corner of Weber Avenue and Center Street in 1847. "In 1847 Bayard Taylor found two log cabins here as the only buildings at this point, erected by Joseph Bussel and John Sirey. [These names are variously spelled.] Bussel's was a tavern, and was patronized by travelers from San Francisco and San Jose. It was torn down in 1850. The logs for these buildings were cut near the asylum, and also about the Mormon slough bulkhead. Where the city now stands was a forest of Oak trees."[133]

During April 1848 between 2,000 and 3,000 people landed in Stockton; Weber was on his way to becoming extremely wealthy. The estimated population of Stockton was two thousand in 1849. A census was not taken in Stockton in 1850, but historians estimated the population to be about

---

[131]Ibid., Page 20.
[132]Lewis Publishing Company, An Illustrated History of San Joaquin County, 1890, Page 67.
[133]Covert Martin, Stockton Album Through the Years, 1959, Page 23.

2,500. In 1850, the streets of Stockton were still a sea of mud in the winter. Residents of the city joked about needing stilts or a boat to cross the streets. Travel by water was much easier during the winter months. Planking was not achieved downtown until 1853; the planking was later replaced by cobblestones from Folsom Prison. "Except for the Baltimore Tent, which was completed in November, 1849, Stockton did not have a regular hotel until the winter of 1849 when the Stockton House was built. It opened for business in the spring of 1850 by the firm Doak, Bonsall, and Scott. The building was of wood, three stories high, and cost about $75,000. When the miners poured into town, they were in too much of a hurry to build log cabins or houses. Who wanted to work as a laborer when he could make from five dollars to one hundred dollars a day mining for gold? Cloth was scarce and high, but it took only a short time to put up a tent. In a few months in 1849 Stockton became a tent city. Some of the buildings had roofs of tule supported by four posts around which canvas had been tacked; much of the canvas was obtained from the sails of the abandoned ships. The Levee was the chief business section. Merchants shipped in goods but could find no building and so set up business on the Levee, or merchants brought in merchandise to ship to the Southern mines, but being unable to find transportation, opened a store in a tent along the Levee. It was only a matter of time until this city, built of such flammable materials, should go up in smoke. The first big fire occurrred on the morning of December 23, 1849. In a few hours' time the business portion of the town bounded by Center, Levee (Weber), Main, and El Dorado streets was completely destroyed by the fire."[134] The first brick had been shipped around Cape Horn from Plymouth, Massachusetts by William Saunders. Captain Weber bought enough of them, in October '49, at one dollar a brick, to make a chimney. Buffum and Cook were merchants who brought a wooden building with

[134]San Joaquin County, History of State of California and Biographical Record of San Joaquin County, 1909, Page 266.

them on the ship, "Eliza"; they erected their store at Weber Avenue east of El Dorado Street.

The town's population had exploded. J.C. Carson wrote in May, 1849, "Stockton that I had last seen graced by Joe Buzzell's log house with a tule roof, was now a vast linen city. The tall masts of the brigs, barks, and schooners, high pointed, were seen in the blue vault above, while the merry yo-ho of the sailors could be heard as box, bale and barrel were landed upon the bank of the slough. The rush and whirl of human beings were constantly before the eye, the magic wand of gold had been shaken over the place and a city had arisen at the bidding of a full fledged Minerva."[135]

"Captain Weber, early in the spring of '49, instructed Richard P. Hammond, a major in the Mexican War and an engineer by profession, to lay out the town. The survey was made of mile square, the blocks being three hundred three feet on each side; seventeen of the blocks were reserved as public squares or breathing places for the people as Captain Weber expresed it. The streets were run along the deep water lines so that the people, for a time, could have free access to navigation. The merchants offered Weber thousands of dollars for water front lots, but he refused to sell at any price. Today is evidenced the great value of an open harbor as a check to the greed of railroads and other corporations."[136]

Weber built the first residence in the valley on what is now the site of a city park and is known as Weber's Point. The walls were made of adobe, which was the material used by the Mexicans; it served as a primitive air-conditioning system: cool in the summer and warm in the winter. The house was finished with polished redwood.

---

[135]Ibid., Page 266.
[136]George Henry Tinkham, California Men and Events, 1915, Page 73.

Stores of every type and description soon popped up in the Levee district: bath houses, stables, watchmakers, jewelers, and merchants who supplied the mining supplies. One of the more notable was Emil Junge's general merchandise store which was located on the store ship 'Susannah', docked in Mormon Slough. Another store was named Ketcham Cheatham, owned by B.F. Cheatham and Thomas E. Ketcham, a lieutenant in the famous Stevenson Regiment. The store was located on the Levee. One night some pranksters changed the sign; the next morning the sign read: "I. Ketcham & U. Cheatham."

One vessel after another sailed up the river and tried to unload more prospectors, more merchandise, and to dock. The ships were too numerous and, "the navigation of the channel was obstructed by the incoming vessels, and in February, 1850, merchants, 107 in number, petitioned Captain Weber to remove the obstructions."[137] In August, 1850, the city was incorporated; soon after Weber deeded all the streets and public squares to the city.

With a population composed mostly of men, and the majority of them being miners, gambling halls soon followed the tents, primitive houses, and taverns. "In 1849, a large gambling tent was standing on the corner of Levee and Center streets, the latter being the principal street in the place. The tent was 100 feet square and contained more than twenty gaming tables. Money and liquor were the chief commodities changing hands here, and amid carousing and all the petty vices connected with such a life. This tent was destroyed by fire May 6, 1851, and in its place was erected another gambling house, known as the El Dorado."[138] Soon another building was erected in 1849 on the southeast corner of Main and Center Streets; it was 30 by 60 feet. This wooden building

[137]Lewis Publishing Company, An Illustrated History of San Joaquin County, 1890, Pages 66-67.
[138]Alta California (newspaper), June 2, 1849, Page 1.

had a floor of imported Oregon pine; a real novelty, it became a saloon and was equipped with the first piano in Stockton. A gambler, Bob Collins, ran gambling tables in the new building. Being a shrewd promoter, he even gave Judge Reynolds a free room upstairs and allowed him to hold court in the saloon. The building was soon to draw a crowd.

For the residents of the city, life was anything but dull. The Alta California paper of June 7, 1849 tells of a quarrel. "A fray at Stockton. A quarrel occurred at Stockton on the 24th May, between an American named Huddart and Jose Jesus, the celebrated Indian chief, in which the latter was shot by the former, the ball entering the right breast, passing upwards, and lodging in the shoulder. At the last advices Jose Jesus was convalescent, and it was thought he would recover, though with the loss of the free use of his right arm. From all accounts, there had been some previous difficulty between the two and they were both intoxicated at the time. Huddart was tried by a jury of twelve men and sentenced to three years confinement in irons. He is to be sent to Gen. Smith to be placed in custody of the military. Huddart was formerly a Lieutenant in the N.Y. Regiment of Volunteers and was honorably discharged at the close of the war. He is a young man of respectable attainments, and it is much to be regretted that he should in a moment of passion thus ruin his prospects and happiness and the hopes of those who are interested in his welfare."[139] It was on the same page of the newspaper that it was announced that a gold coin, struck at Benicia, and bearing the private stamp of "Norris, Greig, & Norris" had come into circulation to ease the shortage of coins. Some of these three men would soon be living in Stockton.

In the 31, 1849, issue of Alta California, Captain Walsh, of Mellus, Howard, & Co. placed an ad for transportation on the s hooner 'Emily and Jane' that would sail to San Francisco on

---

[139]Stockton Historical Society (bulletin), Page 5.

the 10th and 26th of each month from Stockton. The ship could accommodate 30 passengers. On June 7, 1849, the same company announced the arrival of 250 barrels of Columbia River salmon and six barrels of sausage from Oregon.

By summer of 1850 the Stockton House, a new hotel, was opened. The bridge across the Stockton Channel was not finished, but the trestle work was done. At the opening of the hotel,"parties from the business portion of the town walked to the hotel across the stringers. One of the prominent merchants visited the hotel, and made the trip across the stringers of the bridge without accident, but on the return, owing to the fact he was somewhat exhilarated because Stockton was to have a first-class hotel, he missed his footing and walked off into the slough, where the water was over his head."[140]

Financial institutions were also needed, especially banks. "B. Walker Bours opened one of the first banks in California in a canvas structure on Center Street in 1849; it later became the San Joaquin Valley National Bank. The trite expression 'banker's hours' did not hold true in Stockton in the 1850's when banks had long hours and in addition stayed open on Sundays. At this time banks accepted foreign coin based on the aggregate value as determined by a circulation sheet. This problem was created by the fact that only small amounts of United States coins were in circulation."[141]

Captain Weber built the first gold vault in the city in 1851; miners would come in from the mines and could not find a safe place to store their gold. "This vault was placed in his office on the corner of El Dorado and Channel streets. It was built of brick and adobe, but had iron doors which cost $1,000,

[140]George Henry Tinkham, History of San Joaquin County California, 1923, Page 77.
[141]George Henry Tinkham, History of Stockton, 1800, Page 114.

iron at that time being very scarce and high. There he received money, gold dust and valuables of all kinds for safe keeping, charging a certain per cent for the deposit. The following is the exact copy of a receipt given by Weber:

"Received of, Stockton, 18 Aug. 1851, John Beingler, 1 bag containing 4 specimens coarse gold weighing 44 ozs. and two bags containing both together 176 3/4 ozs. gold dust on deposit, depositor paying 1/2 percent per month for safe keeping. Weber & Hammond, Per E.M. Howison."[142]

Todd & Bryan established an express service between Stockton and San Francisco; they would carry packages and letters. Reynolds and Co. Express performed the same function, but in addition, they established routes to all the mines south of the Stanislaus River Their ad read, "Gold dust forwarded through the above expresses - letters taken from the office in San Francisco, Stockton or Sacramento City, and forwarded to all the above mines, and general express business attended to promptly. Office in Stockton with Todd & Bryan."[143] The December 31, 1851, the San Joaquin Republican newspaper announced that plans were proceeding to build a fire-proof brick building. "The masons are aleady at work upon their vault, which will occupy its appropriate place in the brick building; and when completed, will be equal if not superior to any in California, the walls being two feet thick of solid masonry, leaving a space inside of 4 1/2 by 8 feet. We were kindly shown two combination locks intended for the outer and inner doors of this vault which for beauty of finish and as a safeguard for treasure, we have never equalled."[144] The treasure, that the miners worked so hard to acquire, was now

---

[142]Stockton Times (newspaper), May 18, 1850, Page 2.
[143]San Joaquin Republican (newspaper), December 31, 1851, Page 1.
[144]George Henry Tinkham, History of Stockton, 1880, Page 304.

even safer. By November 8, 1851, another express company, Newell and Co., was purchased by Adams & Co.

In these boom times, some businessmen really prospered. "Mr. Zachariah, in 1850, opened a small 6 X 10 clothing store on the levee and invested $50.00 in clothing. From this investment he realized $21,500 in less than six months, went home and returned with his family. He then planted a beautiful orchard and flower garden on the corner of Grant and Park streets, and in 1854 sold his first ripe pears for $3 each."[145]

It wasn't all business and work. There were also good times and tragedies. "In 1849 a ball was given in an adobe house on Main Street below Center. It was quite largely attended, but broke up early, there being only one woman present, and she a Mexican. The presence of a white woman, whether chaste or not, caused a greater excitement and rejoicing than would be caused by the arrival of the Queen of England in our city at the present time. From some defect in society, either socially or otherwise, women have always been a paying feature in saloon, and in the fall of 1849 two women were imported from San Francisco and dealt monte in one of the saloons. It was a sharp transaction, as the women drew crowds to see them and money was freely spent."[146]

Because of the lifestyle and the rugged conditions, tragedies were common. The Stockton Times of April 16, 1850, reported a fatal accident. "On the 17th of February, a fatal accident occurred eight miles from Stockton. A party of young men started from Stockton for the mines, and encamped eight miles from this place. They were six in number J.B. Ridder, C.E.B. Coffin, Stephen Read, John Duffy, and two others. Not having wood enough for the night, Ridder went to cut some, and whilst cutting, his revolver fell out of the holster;

---

[145]Ibid., Page 112.
[146]Stockton Times (newspaper), April 6, 1850, Page 2.

88

the hammer struck on the axe, and the pistol exploded, and, melancholy to relate, the ball entered below the heart of Ridder. The ball was taken out of his back the next morning, but he survived until the next noon. (New York papers will please copy.)"[147]

The population was not isolated because enterprising individuals soon saw the need for more efficient transportation and filled the gap with river steamers on the waterways and stagecoach routes to the various mining communities. One of the first ships was the 'John A. Sutter'; she was making regular trips by September 1849. By June 1850, "the 'Sutter' was withdrawn from the Stockton and placed upon the Sacramento route, having netted her owners the snug little sum of $300,000. While on her way to Marysville a short time afterwards she was blown up, a common fate of steamers in those days, and becoming a total wreck was never rebuilt. The El Dorado took the place of the Sutter upon the Stockton route. The El Dorado was a side wheel steamer. The rate of fare and freight on these two boats was cheap for the times, but was equal to a small fortune at the present, being $20 a ton for freight and $18 cabin passage, or $12 on deck, if the hardy traveler preferred to sleep in his own blankets and was fortunate enough to possess them. A.H. Todd added the ship the 'Mint' to the Stockton run in February, 1850."[148]

On April 11, 1850, the Alta California advertised passage on the "superior fast iron steamer 'Mint' for runs between San Francisco and Stockton, San Joaquin City, Tuolumne and Merced mines. The ship would leave the Central Wharf in San Francisco every Tuesday at 8:00 a.m. The 'Captain Sutter' would leave Stockton for San Francisco every Monday and Thursday at 8:00.

---

[147]George Henry Tinkham, History of Stockton, 1880, Page 319.
[148]George Henry Tinkham, History of San Joaquin County California, 1923, Page 76.

In its February 1, 1851, edition, the Alta California listed seven steamers running between Stockton and San Francisco. They were the 'Union', 'Capt. Sutter', 'El Dorado', 'San Joaquin', 'Erstus Corning', 'Mariposa', and the 'Santa Clara'.

Travel by land was more difficult because of the mud in the rainy season. One newcomer to Stockton summarized the scene, "launches were arriving and departing daily for and from San Francisco and the number of mule-trains, wagons, etc., on their way to various mines with freight and supplies kept up a life of activity truly amazing."[149]

"All the roads from Stockton to the mines were filled with atajos of mules, laden with freight. They were mostly owned by Americans, many of them former trappers and mountaineers, but the packers and driers were Mexican, and the aparejos and alforjas of the mules were of the same fashion at those which, for three hundred years past, have been seen on the hills of Granada and the Andalusian plains."[150]

"In 1850 a Mr. Holden was freighting between Stockton and Sonora, and seeing the large number that were passing and repassing between the two points, concluded to carry lighter freight, make quicker trips, and perhaps, coin more money. So he commenced carrying passengers in his wagon from Stockton to the mines. In the next year this pioneer line was sold to Kelly, Reynolds, & Co. These stages visited all of the mining towns. The longest route was to Mariposa, 110 miles. Two days were required for this trip, and the fare was $20. The best coaches and harnesses were shipped from Concord, New Hampshire, the coaches costing from $1200 to $1500 each."[151]

149Ibid., Page 75.
150George Henry Tinkham, History of Stockton, 1880, Page 313.
151George Henry Tinkham, History of Stockton, 1880, Page

The Stockton Journal published a "Table of Distance" on the various routes. There were three main routes. Calaveras route, Tuolumne route, and the Mariposa route The names of the destinations were as colorful as the newcomers to California: Camp Seco, Chinese Camp, Shaw's Flat (74 miles from Stockton), Yankee Hill, Sweat's Bar, Humbug Creek, Quartzburg, Greaser Gulch, Aqua Frio, and Coarse Gold Gulch. Another list of distances showed that Benicia was 45 miles from San Francisco, and Stockton was 130 miles from the new metropolis on the West Coast, San Francisco.

It was into this bee-hive of activity, progress, and greed that Hiram Norris and his two partners moved sometime in late 1849 or early 1850. The gold was available, the need for coins urgent, to say the least, and the three had proven their ability in Benicia.

315.

Seemingly, never-ending wealth was everywhere. Some of it was being sent back to the eastern states. One early miner described sending some of the gold back home as presents to his family. He related the story, "The package I entrusted to him contained several beautiful specimens of quartz and some gold nuggets, one about the size of small hen's-egg and worth fifty dollars. These I intended for my mother. I also enclosed two slugs or fifty dollars a piece, one for my sister Lucy, and one for my niece, Mary Phipps."[152] Along with the gold, came the element of human greed. The gold never arrived for his family; the messenger claimed that he was robbed during the journey.

Another example of the greed in the mining camps was the process by which miners would rub a little gold off each coin and then spend the coins. In Coulterville, a merchant, Francisco Bruschi, did a lot of business with the Chinese. One evening they bought a sack of $20 gold pieces. "These they took to a cabin hidden up one of the gulches, and placed in a large buck-skin sack. A number of Chinese then kept the sack in motion, for a certain number of hours, timed by a head-man with a clock, and, by ths process, called sweating, wore off part of the gold from each piece. The polished but lighter coins were then returned to him and placed in general circulation."[153] The word finally got out and government officials came and arrested the Chinese; Bruschi had to hide out to avoid arrest.

---

[152]California Historical Quarterly, Volume 6, Page 236.
[153]Newell D. Chamberlain, The Call of Gold: True Tales on the Gold Road to Yosemite, Valley Publishers, 1977, Page 139.

Gold was so plentiful that it was stored, for future use, wherever handy. One miner told of moving into an old, dirty cabin and having to clean it up before taking possession. His partner "found three or four slugs up on a beam in the roof. The previous miner had been in the habit of keeping 'slugs' upon the beam and reaching up for one whenever needed."[154]

On April 1, 1850, the Alta California paper reported problems with accepting California coin and quicksilver gold. A meeting had been held in San Francisco on March 19, 1850, to discuss the problem. In addition, this issue of the paper discussed the problem that spurious gold dust had been shipped from Mexican ports on the steamer, 'California', and the gold had been mixed with quicksilver and dust. The editorial called for immediate investigation of the shipping scheme and for the legislature to do something about the losses resulting from the ever-increasing swindles.

The Monday morning Alta California paper of April 8, 1850, included a long editorial about the problems of attempting to fix the price of gold or the price of California coins. They editorialized that it was impossible to fix the price of any commodity, even gold. They went on to say that, "coin issued by a State is only of the exchangeable value which it represents as long as it keeps up its merchantable value. A debased coin may be made to circulate for a little while, by the arbitrary acts of despotic governments, but it is only for a little while. Gold is a commercial commodity - it is a thing of bargain and sale. It has a value regulated entirely by the market of the world. Any attempt to fix a value upon it higher than it is worth in the market of the world, will be futile. As well might the merchants of Charleston or New Orleans endeavor to fix the price of cotton; the merchants of New York to fix the price of wheat; as the merchants of San Francisco to determine at what

---

[154]California Historical Quarterly, Volume 6, Page 237.

value gold shall be received, what shall be its known, fixed, permanent value in the daily transactions of business."[155]

The April 9, 1851, issue of the Stockton Times wrote about what they called the circulation of irresponsible coin. The article reported, "A considerable amount of this kind of currency is employed in trade, and the sudden depreciation in it affects every dealer. The bankers of San Francisco have refused to receive it, on the grounds that the makers will not redeem it. We think it desirable that our merchants should hold a meeting to determine some uniform rate at which it shall be received in Stockton."[156]

"There were a number of private concerns issuing gold coins at this time, which coins were equal to and in some cases better than, regular United States coins, but they were not legal tender, although accepted as such by the public in its necessity to have a more convenient medium of exchange than gold dust."[157] Edgar Adams stated in his book Private Gold Coinage that, "no less than fifteen establishments in California which from time to time made gold coins for circulation from 1849 to 1855."[158]

Edgar Adams further illuminated the situation. "There was no standard value of gold. It varied in value according to conditions. At the mines and even at certain places along the coast, gold was frequently sold at $6 and $8 an ounce, although worth on an average around $18. There were many instances where it was sold for less, especially by the Indians, who are said to have sold gold-dust as low as a dollar an

---

[155]Alta California (newspaper), April 8, 1850, Page 1.
[156]Stockton Times (newspaper), April 9, 1851, Page 1.
[157]Newell D. Chamberlain, The Call of Gold: True Tales on the Gold Road to Yosemite, Valley Publishers, 1977, Page 33.
[158]Edgar H. Adams, Private Gold Coinage: State Assay Office of California 1850, New York, 1911, Page 3.

ounce, a silver dollar having a real value in their eyes, while they wondered why the white men so highly regarded gold.

All kinds of weights were used, many of them fraudulent. One style of weighing that found favor at the mines was to use two empty sardine boxes as balances, with a silver dollar as an ounce weight. Of course a dollar was a good deal less than an ounce in weight. And there is even record that gold was bought and sold by the avoirdupois ounce."[159]

"The private gold coins made their appearance in 1849. In many instances these private coins soon fell into disrepute as they were worth considerably less than their stamped value, and at one time certain of these pieces were accepted at bullion value only, and were not desirable even then. These coins were accompanied by the general circulation of adulterated gold-dust and bogus nuggets."[160]

Although the establishment of a state assay office was mentioned by July 22, 1848, nothing was done. San Francisco businessmen finally met in April, 1850, to discuss the situation. The business community wanted the state to take over smelting, assaying, and creating gold bars with the state stamp on them. Prior to action by the state, Frederick D. Kohler, who was a jeweler from New York and had been in the gold rush in 1849, established a private assay office in San Francisco. Edgar Adams believed that F.D. Kohler & Co. made the five and ten dollar gold pieces coined by Pacific Company in 1849. Kohler's partner was David C. Broderick with the assay firm of Broderick & Co. Broderick and Kohler had been New York City firemen. Broderick later became a United States Senator and Kohler became the first State Assayer. The State Assay Office continued in business until February 1, 1851, when the United States Assay Office opened.

---

[159]Ibid., Page 5.
[160]Ibid., Page 4.

The gold from California soon found its way back to the mint in Dahlonega, Georgia, where Moffat, another California coiner, had gained invaluable experience. The mint superintendent didn't foresee much gold from California reaching Georgia. "By the middle of 1851, however, he changed his mind about the prospects for the mint. That year, the mint coined far more gold from California than it did from Geogia. While slightly less than $155,000 came from Georgia deposits, more than $214,000 came from California."[161]

The April 5, 1850, Alta California paper published a report regarding the use of pioneer gold coins. Mr. J.J. Cook presided over the meeting of merchants, and John A. Collins, W. J. Sherwood, and E.M. Earl served as secretaries for the gathering. In addition to addressing the question of altered gold dust with quicksilver, the group discussed California coins and wrote the following report: "In addition to 'California Coin' we are clearly of opinion that the interests of the public would be subserved by its universal disuse, for the following reasons:

Because those who receive at par, such even as is honestly made, allow about twelve and one-half per cent, for coinage, estimating gold dust at sixteen dollars per ounce, at the same time that the coin is not legal tender. And here allow us to ask, does the miner, or the community, or the manufacturer realize the enormous profit which is thus made?

Because while we may have full confidence in the stamp of any one or more individuals who issue it, we may not have in another who also issues it, and in whom others may have the same degree of confidence which we have in the case first supposed, thus rendering it extremely difficult to draw a line of distinction between one coiner and another.

---

[161]Sylvia Gailey Head and Elizabeth W. Etheridge, The Neighborhood Mint, Gold Rush Gallery, 2000, Page 164.

Because it has been already the case that coin has been issued which is less valuable at the United States Mint than it purports to be on its face.

Because, as we all know, the redemption of a coin today is not a guarantee that it will be redeemed tomorrow.

Because the issuing of coin has always been considered as one of the highest acts of sovereignty, thus showing that the common experience of mankind is opposed to the issue of private coin.

Because the present abundance of legal coin leaves no occasion for the continuance of a substitute, provided that such a substitute even was necessary or desirable.

The experience of those who have had the most extensive opportunity of knowing, agrees with our own, that the average value of California gold, at the U.S. Mint, after deducting loss by melting, is $17.98/1000 per ounce. The loss by melting averages three per cent. The current value with us, as is well known, has heretofore been $16 per ounce. The difference, which is nearly two dollars per ounce on its Mint value, is, in many cases so much loss to the country, which may be saved to it by proper action on our part. In the action proposed by us, which is to raise the value of gold, assayed and stamped by competent persons, to its value at the U.S. Mint, all classes will certainly be benefited excepting such of us are engaged in the shipment of gold dust on our own account.

One important consideration which should prominently be set forth, is, that this is probably the only course which will put a stop to the issue of private coin, an effect which cannot fail to ensue, as there then will be no profit in its manufacture, unless it is debased. Another consideration is, the fact that, our State, with a Government chosen by ourselves, and on whose action rests the safety of our persons and property, rich in its enlightened population is lamentably in want of funds, for the discharge of pressing liabilities. By the adoption of the course proposed, a very considerable amount of revenue will be derived, scarcely felt by those who contribute to it.

Entertaining the views expressed above, we report the accompanying preamble and resolutions, Joseph J. Cook, for the committee."[162]

In the same issue of the paper, the editor reported reading in the New Orleans Delta paper, dated January 28, 1850, that Mr. Wm. P. Hort, the Assayer of the Mint, described the composition of the recently arrived Mormon coins. He gave testimony that the twenty dollar gold piece had the following in its composition:

> Gold............ 892 parts
> Silver.......... 98 parts
> Unknown.... 10 parts
> Total........... 1000

The controversy continued in Stockton. In the April 6, 1850, edition of the Stockton Times, the editors summarized the situation by saying that all was confusion; neither the state government nor the merchants could come up with an answer. A copy of Editor, John White's article and the H.A. Norris letter appear below.

---

[162]Alta California (newspaper), April 5, 1850, Page 2.

STOCKTON TIMES.

EDITOR—JOHN WHITE.

SATURDAY MORNING, APRIL 6, 1850.

CALIFORNIA GOLD.

One of the most important matters, affecting the welfare of California at the present time is the question of the currency, and yet it is the least understood. Neither our legislature nor our merchants have any settled policy upon which to act: all is confusion and vexation of spirit. It is true the brokers understand to the very cent what are the best terms to trade upon; but no man yet in the country has proposed a plan which shall rescue her from her financial difficulties, and at once reconcile the interests of the vender and the purchaser of goods. The object of the present remarks is, if possible, to some extent to arrest the excitement which exists in this neighborhood in regard to the value of the gold pieces which have been coined in Stockton; so great is this excitement that it is impossible to transact business with them. Now there is not the least reason to doubt that these coins are above par and that they really are what they are stated to be, California Gold without alloy. On this point let Mr. Norris himself speak:

Stockton, 3d April, 1850

DEAR SIR:—In relation to the subject of our conversation a few days since, I will make a few remarks.

1st All the gold coin stamped by me is as it purports on its face to be, of pure placer gold without any admixture of other substances.

2d These coins, on the average, weigh one per cent heavier than the U. S. Half Eagles.

3d I have heard repeatedly and through different channels that these pieces sell readily in the Atlantic cities for one per cent premium. This I have heard with respect to Boston, New York, Philadelphia and New Orleans. Mr. Stephen Bunker has received returns from New York of $800 sent by him in that coin, and it sold at a premium of one per cent. Hon. David J. Douglass, Senator from this district, informed me that some weeks since he saw, in the New Orleans Delta, the result of an essay of one of my pieces at the New Orleans Mint; and that it was found to be worth a few cents above five dollars. Mr. Wm. McSpedon who has recently arrived from New York and who was there engaged in an extensive jewellery house, states that it was a thing well understood among the trade, that the Stockton gold coin was worth from 1 to 2 per cent premium. Mr. J S Freeborn, now of Stockton, who left New York in September last, informs me that he heard from another jewellery establishment of the essay of Stockton gold coins, and that they proved to be of full value. It will certainly be a singular thing if the trading community cannot ascertain the value of these pieces as compared with national coins. And it will be equally strange if the intrinsic value, when ascertained, is not the rate at which they are received in trade.

If I can furnish you with any farther information, I shall be ready to do so.

Very respectfully yours.
H A NORRIS.

100

On April 11, 1850, the Alta California newspaper carried an editorial by J.J.C. followed by a letter from a writer named Zeno. A copy of the editorial and Zeno's letter appear below:

[COMMUNICATED.]

MESSRS. EDITORS:—The appearance of an article in your paper signed "N." compels me, very reluctantly, again to ask of you the privilege of a small space in your columns, in order that however erroneous and ill advised the report of the committee on the currency question may truly have been, they may not be condemned as being guilty of absurdities for which they are not in the least degree responsible. That the "Report" should be made to suffer for every cupidity which may enter into the mind of any individual, appears to me to be very unfair. In other articles which have been published in relation to the subject, this has been, (however unintentionally on the part of the writers,) the case to some extent. In the article now under consideration, the author almost directly charges the Report with proposing an "expedient" to "substitute bills of exchange for remittances," which may have had no other existence than in his own imagination, as it is certainly not to be found in the "Report." The committee do not need to have "N." admonish them that debts must be paid, although he has the privilege of sneering at their "patriotism and justice." How will he make his remittances after a legal mint shall have been established. or must debts then remain unpaid? The price of gold dust will then surely be enhanced.

The present writer apprehends that the real "value of gold dust in California," as in all other parts of the world, is exactly what it is worth in exchange for "breeches, boots and shoes, sugar or coffee," (and such other articles as are wanted by man) and also that, if "N." will investigate the subject, he will find that this is the real "value" of "the coin of the United States and of that of other countries."

"The conventional value here," has a "bearing upon the quantity to be exported," just so far as men who act from what is merely apparent, are governed in disposing of their gold dust by the nominal value, and also so far as it is exported to pay for coin, to be used unnecessarily as currency.

The author of the report in question is not tenacious of the price of gold dust, but he is desirous of being correctly represented. It is an easy matter to assume that certain arguments are those of others; leaving innocent parties to bear the obloquy, which may be the consequence, provided that such a course is allowed to pass unnoticed.   J. J. C.

Alta Calif. April 11, 1850 **Currency.**

Currency.

Private issues of paper, silver, or gold, *as currency*, ought to be discountenanced. A good issue, *as currency*, is no better than paper if it is not redeemable where it circulates, at par, in American gold coin. A depreciation in the substitutes for currency, subjects the holders to inconvenience and loss. That loss is generally sustained by working men, and therefore the evil is greater than if it were confined to capitalists.

The issue of the "Miner's Bank" is a drug in the market. Brokers refuse to take it at less than twenty per cent. discount. Moffat's issue will probably soon be no better; he already refuses to redeem it in American gold coin. Those who have it would do well to get five franc pieces to the dollar which is really seven per cent discount for it, at Moffat's counter now, as it is not impossible they may refuse to pay even that for it soon.

Working men as a matter of interest ought to refuse all such spurious issues. The rich ought to reject them on the ground of principle and for the general good. None but those who make such issues know their intrinsic value; and when they refuse to redeem their own money in American gold coin, it is but fair to conclude that their "California Gold" is a gross deception.   ZENO.

San Francisco, April 10, 1850.

Two days later the Stockton Times reported on the currency meeting that had been held in San Francisco. Below is a copy of their summary.

Saturday Morning, April 13, 1850.

CURRENCY MEETING AT SAN FRANCISCO——CALIFORNIA COIN.

Last week, a "highly respectable gathering of the merchants" of San Francisco occurred to take into consideration the reform long agitated in the community in regard to the value of gold coin and dust.

The object of the meeting appears to have been, 1st to secure the universal disuse of "California coin," 2d to secure the universal disuse of "quicksilver gold" as currency; 3d to recommend the legislature to appoint an assayer, whose "ingots, stamped by him, with the fineness, weight, and U. S. Mint value" shall be received at par in all our business transactions; and 4th, "to receive gold dust in payment in its natural form at $17 per ounce.

The principcipal reason for the disuse of California coin is set forth thus :

" Because those who receive at par, such even as is honestly made, allow about twelve and one half per cent, for coinage, estimating gold dust at sixteen dollars per ounce, at the same time that the coin is not a legal tender. And here allow us to ask, does the miner, or the community, or the manufacturer realise the enormous profit which is thus made?"

The manufacturer, certainly. We quite agree with the committee that it is a highly dangerous principle to leave the coinage of gold in the hands of irresponsible parties.— But why this sneer at the manufacturer? Why have these merchants delayed until this period the exhibition of their "patriotism and justice?" We learn from the report of the director of the United States Mint that our gold dust after melting is worth $18,50, whereas the market price in San Francisco is only $16, and here " allow us to ask" "does the miner, or the community, or do the merchants who are on the committee realize the enormous profit which is thus made?"

103

The manufacturer, certainly. We quite agree with the committee that it is a highly dangerous principle to leave the coinage of gold in the hands of irresponsible parties.— But why this sneer at the manufacturer? Why have these merchants delayed until this period the exhibition of their "patriotism and justice?" We learn from the report of the director of the United States Mint that our gold dust after melting is worth $18,50, whereas the market price in San Francisco is only $16, and here "allow us to ask" "does the miner, or the community, or do the merchants who are on this committee realize the enormous profit which is thus made?"

California coin may fall into disuse, not because of dishonest practices on the part of the principal manufacturers, ... that both Moffat's and Nor-.......coins are worth the sum which they

.... more effectual laws by the Congress of the United States. Now it occurs to us that the matter will not be much mended by the appointment by the Legislature of assayers whose ingots are to take the place of the coins at present in circulation. Ingots may be fit articles for exportation, but an ingot is certainly very unfit as a medium of exchange in regard to the internal commerce of the country. These gentlemen will next be proposing that we return to the days of good old Isaac and Jacob, when as the song says, " money was all in lumps." We submit that as this is purely a mercantile affair, the question should be settled by the merchants themselves. It would have been far wiser had these merchants of San Francisco resolved that none but coins manufactured by Mr. Moffat (whose experience and skill render him worthy of trust) shall be received as currency; than to have resolved that we should carry ingots in our pockets instead of coins, and then to run their head against one of the columns of political economy and proclaimed that gold dust should henceforward be worth $17 per ounce.

By April 15, 1850, a Mr. E. Sprague wrote a letter to the local paper, the Stockton Times, supporting the Norris coin. Sprague's letter is copied below:

MR. NORRIS' COIN.

Mr. Editor :—The interests of the community being affected by all monetary changes I feel it due to this section that they be not injured by deception. Mr. Norris came among us without flourish of trumpets a large parade, to do a safe and healthful business; his success is known to those who have inquired. Whether he deserves the countenance and support of the people depends on the wants of the public, and his qualifications to supply them.

That a circulating medium is demanded can be denied by none, and that specie will not be imported to this state of sufficient amount to accommodate the business men of the state is tested by every weighing of gold dust. If so a circulating medium of sufficient magnitude is demanded. To meet this command, is Mr. Norris' coin equal, and of its value? That it would answer in quantity would depend on the amount made. So far as he might go so far answered.

Then is it par value? It has been assayed at the New Orleans Mint, and pronounced "one per cent premium;" a large amount has also been assayed by Mr. Moffat at San Francisco, and pronounced "good." I have weighed considerable against U. S. coin and his was heaviest in every case. Is it then alloyed? This can be tested by any one by comparing the size of the pieces. His is invariably the smallest—if smallest and heaviest then the purest—if the purest then the most valuable—if the most valuable then worthy of confidence. I abominate imposition come from whom it may, and is it not an imposition to stop his coin and reduce its value? That it is not as heavy as the dust is true, else he would not coin it; but is it not as *valuable?* Gold dust is cheaper here than in the older states, because of its abundance and distance from the mint. This coin then is just what alone can meet the wants of the public.

Who then, is opposed to its circulation? the people are not—the merchants pretend to be desirous to have it pass. None then but the brokers are against it. Should the people submit to it? The brokers have their use, but should they control my interests to my injury and their emolument? No person of right principles would submit to it for a moment. If so, what is our duty? Not to make war but to assert rights. The merchant must sell his goods—he cannot sell unless he takes my pay. If I have Mr. N's coin and he will not take it, let him keep his goods; Let all the people say thus and the controversy is ended; we are not swindled out of fifty cents in five dollars either. I would suggest that some public action be had on this matter and that our interests and convenience be consulted as well as the brokers. Yours, &c.,

Stockton, April 15.   E. SPRAGUE.

———o———

The Stockton Times further fueled the controversy. On May 25, 1850, they quoted the New York Tribune to describe the tremendous amounts of gold being received by the mints. The Washington Mint had received $8,500,000 of California gold dust up until February 28, 1850; and from the 1st to the 15th of March, 1850, they had received an additional $825,000 of gold dust. Meanwhile, the New Orleans Mint had received $1,901,102 of California gold dust. The Tribune estimated that almost $2,000,000 more in gold dust was still in private hands. The article went on to say, "The coinage at the mint during the present quarter has been very heavy, as may have been inferred from the number of certificates paid. About $100,000 of double eagles have been coined and issued, and a still larger amount will be coined in the course of a few days.

There is no inconsiderable amount of circulation of the coinage of the private mints of California. They are not worth the value represented. The $20.00 Mormon pieces are now worth only from $17.53 to $17.88; the $10.00 from $8.50 to $8.70; the $5 about $4.30; the $2.50 about $2.25.   The California $5 coins range in value from $4.82 up as high as $5.96. The $10 about $9.60. They are, therefore, all of less value than the coins of the United States."[163]

To further complicate matters, by June 15, 1850, the Stockton Times was reporting the appearance of counterfeit coins, of the eagle, half-eagle, and quarter-eagle denominations. The coins were of sufficient weight, but they were composed of a thin planchet of Spanish silver and overlayed with a thin layer of gold plate.

Almost a year later, on April 2, 1851, the Stockton Times printed a very interesting appraisal of several California gold coins. James King of Williams had sent a selection of coins to the U.S. Assayer to be evaluated. A lot of the coins were not of full value. The paper summarized the results, "From which it

---

[163]Stockton Times (newspaper), May 25, 1850, Page 2.

would appear that on each of the twenty dollar pieces the holder would lose sixty cents, should he present them to the mint, or three percent; on the tens the loss would be twenty-six cents, or nearly the same per centum. The class of coins named last in the list of Mr. King, (Dubosq's) appears to approach most nearly to the United States mint standard value, the loss being only seven-tenths of one per cent, or seven cents on ten dollars, while that of Baldwin is three per cent, or thirty cents on ten dollars."[164]

---

[164]Stockton Times (newspaper), April 2, 1851, Page 1.

Who were these three men who have been given historical credit for producing the Norris, Gregg, & Norris coins? First, we need to focus on the time period between November 13, 1848, when members of the Mormon Battalion arrived in the Great Salt Lake Valley carrying gold dust; and April 20, 1850, when the State Assay Office was created by law. This assay office preceded the establishment of the U.S. Assay Office in San Francisco; the U.S. office did not begin operations until February 1, 1851. The Norris, Gregg, & Norris party probably ceased the minting of their coins by April 20, 1850.

The "Utah Early Records" have this to say: "On the 13th of November, 1848, fifteen Battalion men arrived from California. During the month several other small companies arrived. Some of them brought considerable gold dust with them. On the 19th of November 1848, preparation was made to make coin of the gold dust brought back from California. On the 25th Brigham Young, John Taylor and John Kay (a blacksmith) made out an inscription for the gold currency...on one side "Holiness to the Lord" with an emblem of the Priesthood. On the reverse the words "Pure Gold: and the coin, surrounding two hands clasped, representing friendship."[165]

Bancroft, a noted California historian says that, "the dies and everything connected with the coining were made in Salt Lake City, but that the crucibles broke and for the time being the attempt to coin money was abandoned."[166]

---

[165]Reva Holdaway Stanley, The First Utah Coins Minted From California Gold, California Historical Society Quarterly, Volume 15, September 1936, Page 244.
[166]Ibid., Page 244.

An entry for April of 1849 in the 'Records' says: "On the return of a portion of the Mormon Battalion through the northern part of Western California, they discovered an extensive gold mine, which enabled them, by a few days' delay, to bring sufficient of the dust to make money plenty in this place, for all ordinary purposes of public convenience, in the exchange the brethren deposited the gold dust with the Presidency, who issued bills, or a paper currency."[167]

"A few months later, a second attempt was made to coin gold, which this time was attended with more success. J.M. Barlow, a jeweler, was requested by Brigham Young to make a set of dies for $5 pieces, and for a number of years he refined the gold and coined it into money. Coins of $2.50, $10, and $20 were also minted, although by whom is not of record."[168]

It seems probable that pioneer gold coins were coined as early as November of 1848. It would be almost certain that by April of 1849 a substantial number of coins were produced on the Utah frontier. A newspaper account of May 31, 1849, first mentioned the Norris, Gregg, & Norris coin, and described the appearance of the coin, which was struck in Benicia, but bore the imprint of San Francisco.

---

[167]Ibid., Page 244.
[168]Ibid., Page 245.

The California private gold coins made their appearance in 1849; some private territorial gold coins had been minted in Salt Lake, probably in 1848. "There were two general methods used in the striking of the California gold pieces. In at least two cases known, Pacific Company and J.S. Ormsby Company, the coins were produced with the power from a sledge hammer as the force to cause the metal to flow into the design of the dies. For this system, equipment used by these concerns was similar to that used by the Oregon beaver coins, which dies are still preserved by the Oregon Historical Society.

Blank slugs, or planchets, are fed into the space between the dies. The steel collar prevents the coin from spreading. The friction from the blow causes the metal to soften and flow into the valleys of the dies."[169]

"The second method of manufacturing the coins was by the use of a screw press. This press was either powered by hand or with the use of steam. The screw press is the one used by the Bechtlers in Georgia just before the California gold rush. It is not at all improbable that many of the California mints used presses like this."[170]

The situation soon became confusing. The Alta California newspaper had reported on May 31, 1849, that Norris, Gregg, & Norris had produced a gold coin bearing their initials in Benicia City, but with a San Francisco imprint. By 1850 some, or all, of the Norris party had moved to Stockton. About the same time a Moffat coin had begun to circulate.

---

[169]Bryan O. Burke Jr., California Pioneer Gold Coins, Masters Thesis, The University of Redlands, 1963, Page 18.
[170]Ibid., Page 19.

Early in 1849 the Norris, Gregg & Norris coins appeared in California. These coins were all $5.00 gold pieces. Bancroft wrote, "Several private establishments began to coin money. At first rectangular bars worth $20 and $50; then gold pieces of $2.50, $5, $10, $20, $25 and $50, resembling national coins, with eagles and other designs, but bearing the name of the coiners, and usually the initials S.M.V. - 'standard mint value' - although mostly somewhat below this. The alloy was generally silver, which imparted a brassy tint. The Philadelphia mint reported in 1851 upon the coinage of fifteen private California mints, with from one to four denominations of coin each. 1. A neatly executed coin marked N.G.&N., with an eagle encircled in stars, and the late San Francisco 1849; on the reverse. 'California gold without alloy' very nearly sustained its claim to the full weight of a half-eagle, assaying without the silver, which constituted 2.5 percent, from $4.83 to $4.89."[171]

There were only three varieties of N.G.&N. coins. In 1849, the coiners made a $5.00 gold piece with a plain edge; they also made a $5.00 gold piece with a reeded edge in the same year. Both of these varieties had the imprint 'San Francisco' on them. In 1850, the coiners made a third variety of the $5.00 gold coin, with the imprint 'Stockton' on the reverse. To the author's knowledge only one coin exists with the word Stockton on it; this coin was discovered in the 1940's. It is the author's opinion, after seven years of research, that the Norris, Gregg, & Norris coiners made only these three varieties. The one known, existing 1850 coin is in the National Numismatic Collection in the Smithsonian.

Jacob R. Eckfeldt and William E. DuBois, in their 1851 book, 'New Varieties of Gold and Silver Coins' described the N.G.&N. coin thusly, "The N.G.&N. does not profess the same degree of accuracy as Bechtler's, as to fineness...the legend on the reverse, CALIFORNIA GOLD WITHOUT ALLOY, allows

_____

[171]Herbert Howe Bancroft, History of California, Volume VII, Page 165.

a pretty wide range. As far as our assays go, the truth of this stamp is proved there is no alloy other than that already introduced by the hand of nature, and which is generally more than sufficient. Three pieces gave severally the fineness of 870, 880, and 892 thousandths; all were within the scope of California gold. They consequently are worth $4.83, $4.89, and $4.95 respectively, without the silver; and including that 2.5 cents more. The coin is neatly executed, and, beside the two legends above quoted, bears an eagle, a circle of stars, the date 1849, and the name San Francisco. It wears the somewhat brassy tint which belongs to gold alloyed with silver only."[172]

Nationally renowned coin expert, Donald H. Kagin, in his 1981 book, stated that historian Edgar H. Adams believed that the N.G.&N. coin was the first California gold coin. Mr. Kagin also stated, "historian Edgar H. Adams claims they were the first on the grounds that they were the first coiners to be cited in the California newspapers. The firm is also the first company mentioned in Eckfeldt and DuBois' book, New Varieties of Gold and Silver Coins (1850). Some private gold coiners, however, never were cited in California papers. Any one of them could have issued products prior to those from Norris, Gregg, and Norris. There is a possibility that Bowie & Company and Meyers & Company might have preceded Norris, Gregg, & Norris."[173]

The September 15 and September 27, 1849, issues of Alta California included an announcement signed by Moffat & Co. It read: "GOLD COIN - Messrs Moffat & Company announce to the people of California that they have constructed the requisite machinery, and secured the services

---

[172]Jacob R. Eckfeldt and William E. DuBois, New Varieties of Gold and Silver Coins, 1851, Page 7.
[173]Donald H. Kagin, Phd., Private Gold Coins and Patterns of the United States, Arco Publishing, Inc., New York City, 1981, Page 62.

of an experienced and skillful engineer from the United States Mint, and are about issuing a coinage of the denominations of five and ten dollars. They [the] design their coin shall be struck and accurately in accordance with that of the United States Mint, in fineness, weight, color, value, and mechanical execution. For their integrity, and ability to accomplish their intentions, they confidently refer to their credentials below. All coin issued to them will be redeemable at their counter in silver."[174]

Thus by September of 1849, at least two or more companies were producing gold coin. The coin crisis was being temporarily solved. Finally, the vast quantity of gold-dust was being turned into a readily usable form.

---

[174]Alta California (newspaper), September 15 and September 27, 1849, Page 1.

Who were these three coiners, who may have been the first to solve the coinage problem in California? It took three businessmen from Brooklyn, New York, to provide an early answer to the shortage of coins. Finally, in 1849, the three provided a means to conveniently use the tremendous amounts of gold-dust that were flowing into the communities.

The three coiners were businessmen; their business, in the New York Directory of 1849, was described as a manufacturing company which produced iron pipes and fittings for all kinds of steam, water, gas, etc. Thomas H. Norris and Hiram A. Norris were both civil engineers who owned the business at 62 Gold Street in Brooklyn. Their other partner was Charles Gregg, also an engineer at the same business location. Thomas lived at 68 Jay Street in Brooklyn, while Hiram lived at 310 Gold Street, also in Brooklyn. Charles Gregg lived at 209 Pearl Street in Brooklyn. All of these addresses are within 3 or 4 blocks of each other.

Evidentally one, two, or maybe all three of them had journeyed to San Francisco. In the November 17, 1849 issue of the Pacific News there appeared a list of mail that had not been collected in the San Francisco Post Office. The 'advertised' letters had been waiting a minimum of three months in the post office. On this list is the name of Thomas Norris. It would seem that someone had expected Thomas Norris to be in San Francisco by August 17, 1849; the date by which the letter would have had to arrive. This newspaper notice is on page 4, Volume 1, No. 37.

Donald Kagin correctly speculates that the Norris, Gregg, & Norris party soon left Benicia, where the first coin was made. He states, "It is now believed that Norris, Gregg, & Norris moved to Stockton from Benicia sometime in 1850. One source states that an A. Reimers of San Francisco, a close friend of Mr. Kuner, told some coin collectors that Kuner insisted that Norris, Gregg, & Norris were businessmen in Stockton. Significantly, in 1947, a specimen was found with the word "Stockton" on the die and dated 1850. This piece might very well have been made after Norris, Gregg, & Norris moved from Benicia to Stockton. An article in the Stockton Times of April 6, 1850, mentions the presence of a coining operation of Norris, Gregg, & Norris in Stockton."[175]

It is the author's belief that the April 20, 1850, date is extremely significant; it was both the date of the letter of controversy, written by E. Sprague in the Stockton Times about the Norris, Gregg, & Norris coin, and the date of the creation of the State Assay Office by California law.

In searching the New York Directories from 1848 until 1861, the author found that the business was named the Norris, Gregg, & Norris Company. From 1848, or earlier, until 1853, the company's name included the three names; however, form 1853 until the 1861 Directory, the company was named Norris & Gregg. The business was located at 62 Gold Street in 1848-49 and 1849-50, but their business address included 64 Gold Street until 1855. In the 1855-56 Directory they were located at 62 Gold Street and 67 Beekman Street. In 1857-58 they were located at all three addresses. In 1858-59, they listed only 62 Gold Street and 67 Beekman Street as their place of business. The Directory of 1859-60 listed their address as all three locations again, but the 1860-61 Directory only listed 64 Gold Street as their location. They listed their business as 'iron pipes' in every directory except 1859-60 when they recorded their business as 'gas fittings'.

From the available information, the author surmises that the company stayed in business during the time of the gold rush. The name change in 1853 coincides with the death of

---

[175]Donald H. Kagin, Private Gold Coins & Patterns of the United States, 1981, Page 64.

Hiram Norris on August 12, 1853; the company must have continued with Thomas Norris and Charles Gregg as the partners. Another interesting recording is that they expanded the business to 64 Gold Street in 1850, the last year that they made coins.

In searching the New York Directories for information on Hiram Norris' residence, it was discovered that he listed his occupation as civil engineer in 1848-1850. In the 1850-51 Directory there isn't any listing for him. In 1851, 52 and 53 he lists iron pipes as his business. He gives his home as being located at 310 Gold Street in 1848, 1849 and 1850; there, of course, isn't a listing for 1850-51, and from then until his death he listed 88 Johnson Street as his address in Brooklyn.

Thomas H. Norris maintained the same business address on Gold Street, but never listed the address on Beekman Street. In 1848, he listed his business as mason. In 1849 and 1850, he listed his business as merchant. From 1851, he lists his business as iron pipe dealer, except for 1856 when he listed his occupation as merchant. He described his business as gas fittings for the first time in 1860. Thomas resided at 268 Jay Street from 1848 until 1853. In 1853 he lived on Green Avenue; from 1854 until 1857 his residence was Washington and Gates Avenue. In 1857-58, he lived on Gates Avenue and Glasson. In 1859 and 1860 he resided on Gates Avenue near Franklin.

About the time that Norris, Gregg, & Norris traveled west to put their names in the history book of numismatics, John L. Moffat, also of Brooklyn, left for San Francisco and the gold rush. He was an experienced assayer and geologist and had spent many years in the Georgia gold fields. Moffat "went to California early in 1849, and in the summer of that year opened a smelting and assaying business in conjunction with Messrs. Joseph R. Curtis, P.H.W. Perry, and Samuel H. Ward. They did an extensive gold brokerage business at Clay and Dupont

Streets, in connection with their work of assay, and purchased much gold-dust, which they shipped to the east."[176]

An early advertisement of Moffat & Co. appeared in the Alta California paper on September 6, 1849. Thus, the Norris, Gregg, & Norris group was documented as being in business in May of 1849, and Moffat & Co. was in business by September of 1849. And, they were all from Brooklyn. Had they known each other in New York before the gold rush? They all knew Albert Kuner! The advertisement carried an endorsement for Moffat, and the quality of his assay-stamp; it was dated New York, Feb. 7, 1849, and signed by Beebe, Ludlow & Co.

Moffat issued small bars of gold with his stamp on them; they were much more convenient to use than gold dust. The ingots were probably issued in June or July, 1849. "They answered the purpose for which they were made fairly well, but the arrival of Albert Kuner at San Francisco, on July 16 made their further issue unnecessary. Mr. Kuner, a Bavarian, had come to America as a cameo cutter, but upon his arrival at San Francisco was at once employed by Moffat & Co. to cut the dies for a ten-dollar piece. This ten-dollar piece, which followed closely the general design of the United States eagle, bore as distinguishing marks the name of 'Moffat & Co.' on the coronet of Liberty, instead of the word 'Liberty', as shown on the issues of the General Government."[177]

"A short time after the 1849 ten-dollar piece was issued by Moffat & Co., they struck a five-dollar piece. This coin was similar to the larger denomination, and the dies were also made by Mr. Kuner. In 1850 Moffat & Co. struck gold coins of the denomination of five dollars only. This piece was similar in design to that of 1849, with the exception of the date. It was also a product of the skill of engraver Kuner. These pieces

---

[176]Edgar H. Adams, Private Gold Coinage, Part II, 1911, Page 13.
[177]Ibid., Page 15.

were struck in great numbers, as is evidenced by their comparative abundance even at the present time.

The year 1850 brought to an end the operations of many of the private mints, but Moffat & Co.'s establishment was advanced from a private mint to a semi-official mint."[178]

Who was Mr. John Moffat? In his autobiography, John S. Diltz, an early miner in Mariposa, California, remembers Moffat: "Mr. Moffat, of Brooklyn, New York, was out there and he and my uncle ran together for several years in their mineralogical and geological explorations. In 1848, General Taylor was elected President and in 1849 my uncle was appointed Assayer in the Dahlonega, Georgia Branch Mint, and old Mr. Moffat was appointed in San Francisco. His Assay office was in a large fireproof building on Commercial Street and in the time of the great fire, he was shut up in the building. It got so hot in there, he went down in the basement and threw himself on the ground and lay there till all the surrounding buildings were burned and when he got up, he found the great iron doors red hot and warped and drawn so out of shape that the air got in through the cracks and consequently saved the old man's bacon. Later, he sold out to Kellogg and Company and shipped most of his money home. He then interested some parties in his mine, got machinery and took it up to Mt. Ophir, where they spent money foolishly in putting up pulleys and ropes, with cars attached, to run ore from the top and the loaded car to draw up the empty one.

In the latter part of 1851, I got ready to come out to Mr. Moffat. I leased my mine, early in 1852 and started for another land of gold. Mr. Moffat sold out and was then on the San Joaquin River, building boats and diving bells to get the sands and gold from the river bed. I stayed with him during the

---

[178]Ibid., Page 17.

summer of 1852 and I concentrated black sand for them, while Dr. Wooster was superintending the submarine work."[179]

Mt. Ophir is located in Mariposa County on Highway 49 in California. John Moffat had both mining interests and minting interests on, and near, Mt. Ophir. He had filed a mining claim on Mt. Ophir, which he operated alone at first and then in association with an incorporated company, the Merced Mining Company. It was this mine that supplied the gold used in the first fifty dollar slugs, made by him in his mint at Mt. Ophir, and these were the first coins issued in California under governmental authority. Moffat's Mint at Mt. Ophir, therefore, was really the nation's first authorized private mint.

Local historical writings describe the mint at Mt. Ophir. The background for this coin is best told by Newell Chamberlain, "Nesting along a hillside, among scrub oaks, in a lightly elevated clearing near the base of Mt. Ophir, Mariposa County, is located Moffat's Mint. This was built of local slate rock, in 1850, by John L. Moffat, who had been appointed the year previously by President Zachary Taylor as U.S. Assay for California, at which time, he established an assay office on Commercial Street, in San Francisco"[180] (The author located the ruins of this slate mint building in the forest of oaks in March, 2000.) There are two good photographs of the slate mint building in the Master's Thesis written by Bryan O. Burke, Jr., in June of 1963; this thesis is available in the University of Redlands Library in Redlands, California.

In the county courthouse in Mariposa, there are several documents bearing John Moffat's name and signature. They are located in Book 1, pages 102, 104, 107, 296, and 298. On page 422 in Book 1 there are court dealings on December 5, 1851, for the Merced Mining Co., in which Moffat was involved.

---

[179]Newell D. Chamberlain, The Call of Gold; True Tales on the Gold Road to Yosemite, Valley Publishers, 1977, Page 93.
[180]Ibid., Page 33.

In addition, there are location notices on pages 81 and 82 of Location Notices. There are also Moffat's fillings in the Quartz Records on pages 1, 2, 76, 77, and 78.

The mystery remains. How were Kuner, Moffat, and Norris, Gregg, & Norris connected? This author feels that at least they were acquaintances, if not friends!

The mystery of who carved the dies for the N.G.& N. $5.00 coin bearing the words 'San Francisco' is an ongoing mystery. For many years the significance of the letters 'N.G.& N' was a mystery.   In 1902 the coins of Augustus Humbert were sold; among them was an uncirculated N.G.&N. $5.00 coin wrapped in paper bearing the words, "From my friends, Norris, Grigg, & Norris."[181]

Edgar Adams goes on to state, "Albert Kuner is credited with having engraved the dies for this coin - or, at least for one bearing the stamp of Norris, Grieg, & Norris. As he was unusually painstaking and methodical, it is difficult to imagine that he was wrong when he stated that he had engraved the dies. One would rather think that there had been another variety. As Mr. Kuner did not arrive in San Francisco until July 16, 1849, he could not have engraved the dies in question. It is well known that the Five Dollar piece of Norris, Gregg, and Norris is entirely and radically different in design from any coin ever produced at the United States Mint. The only resemblance would be in the size. We may reasonably assume that the correct spelling of the name of the second member of the firm should be Grieg, as given in the newspaper of 1849, rather than Grigg, as spelled on the wrapper of Humbert's coin."[182]

George Ferdinand Albrecht Kuner was from Lindau, Bavaria; he was born on October 9, 1819. In Europe he had learned the trades of goldsmith and silversmith, and he was a talented cameo cutter. Because business was bad, he left

---

[181]Edgar H. Adams, Private Gold Coinage III: Various Californian Private Mints 1849-1855, New York, 1912, Page 66.
[182]Ibid., Page 66.

Germany for New York, on September 3, 1848, on the ship 'Swyzerland.' He did well for a time, but the gold news from California lured him to California on the ship 'Sutton' on January 1, 1849. Kuner stated, "We had had hopes of spending the Fourth of July in San Francisco, but in this we were badly disappointed, for the weather changed and so did the wind. So we did not get there until the twenty-second of July."[183]

Thus, there is a discrepancy between the July 22 date quoted by Adams and the January 1, 1849 date of departure. If the ship the 'Sutton' operated only on the Pacific Coast, it would not have taken 6 months of travel up the coast. He soon found employment with Moffat & Co.'s Assaying Office on the southeast corner of Jackson and Montgomery Streets. The company was owned by Jos. R. Curtis, manager; S.H. Ward, secretary; P.H. Perry, cashier: and John L. Moffat, assayer. Kuner, in his autobiography, said, "The first piece of work I had to do in California was to engrave a set of steel dies for a ten dollar piece. Of course, I took great pains to do my work well, and I met with great success, giving perfect satisfaction to my employers. Then I started on a set of five dollar dies, which were also completed satisfactorily. The coins were put into circulation, if I remember rightly, in the latter part of August. I had all the work I could do as there were by now two establishments in the 'Assaying and Coining' business, and there were lots of seals to engrave."[184] Thus, he arrived in California during the gold rush, and set up a business by October 1849 on Clay Street in San Francisco. In California, he dropped his first two names and went by the name of Albert. It is known that he engraved the dies for the Moffat & Co. $10.00 gold piece. Sadly, a lot of his records, wax models, and

---

[183]George Albrecht Ferdinand Kuner, Autobiography of George Albrecht Ferdinand Kuner, The Society of California Pioneers Annual Bulletin (1944), Page 25.
[184]Ibid., Page 26.

dies were destroyed in a series of three fires that he suffered both at his business and his home.

According to Edgar H. Adams in his 1913 book, one very valuable document survived. Adams states, "However, a record of many of the coins for which he cut the dies remains in his personal copy of the book issued by Eckfeldt & DuBois in 1851. He made a memorandum in his own handwriting over each illustration of the various California coins engraved by him. Guided by these notes we find that he made the dies of the N.G.&N. Five Dollar piece, the Five and Ten Dollars of Moffat & Co. dated 1849 and 1850; the Schultz & Co. Five Dollars of 1851, the Dunbar & Co. Five Dollars dated 1851; the Baldwin Five, Ten, and Twenty Dollars of 1850 and 1851; and the Fifty Dollar octagonal, with the denomination reading, 'Fifty Dolls.' and the name on the obverse around the border.

The illustrations of the Miners' Bank Ten Dollars, the Pacific Company Five and Ten, the Massachusetts and California Five, the Templeton Reid Ten and Twenty-five, the Cincinnati Mining and Trading Company Five and Ten, the 'J.S.O.' Ten and the Dubosq & Co. Five and Ten Dollar coins were not marked, and therefore were not his work."[185]

The arrival of Albert Kuner in San Francisco was on the date of July 16, 1849. The mystery is that the N.G.N. coin was in existence by May 31, 1849. As Adams relates, "Of course it is possible that he cut the N.G.& N. dies before he got to that city."[186]

As a sidelight, the book, The History of San Francisco, summarizes the life of Rev. Herman Gehrcke, who had been born in Germany on October 15, 1865. He had come to California in 1891 and was an ordained Lutheran minister.

---

[185]Edgar H. Adams, Private Gold Coinage III: Various Californian Private Mints 1849-55, New York, 1912, page 93.
[186]Ibid., Page 95.

Rev. Gehrcke was married to Miss Martha Kuner, a native of California and was "the daughter of Albert Kuner, who was born in Bavaria and came to California in 1849. He was a noted engraver, and had the distinction of having engraved the state seal of California. He won fame by his cameo engravings and was in every way an accomplished artist."[187] In 1932 Rev. and Mrs. Gehrcke were the parents of three children; two were still living: Albert L.H. and Helen, the wife of Ernest Conradi.

---

[187]History of San Francisco, Page 461.

Where did Thomas Norris, Hiram Norris, and Charles Gregg go after the gold rush? What happened to them after the month of April 1850, when Hiram Norris had written his letter in support of Norris, Gregg, & Norris coins in the Stockton Times? Neither of the Norris brothers, nor Charles Gregg's name appears in the 1852 'Stockton Directory & Emigrant's Guide to the Southern Mines'. It was published by the San Joaquin Republican office in 1852. Nor do any of their names appear in the 1856 Stockton Directory. None of the three were members of the Stockton Club in 1850. Another place to which we can turn is to the real estate records of San Joaquin County, in Stockton; the records are well preserved, but some of the handwriting of that era is difficult to decipher.

A search of real estate transactions during the years of 1849, 1850 and 1851 in the San Joaquin County Courthouse, in Stockton, revealed three transactions involving the three coiners; the only name of the three that appears in the legal records is that of Hiram A. Norris. Was he the leader of the three?

On April 9, 1850, H.A. Norris was the grantor in a land transaction with E.M. Howison, who conducted a lot of Charles Weber's business transactions (located in Book A of G, page 451).

On May 1, 1850, Charles M. Weber signed an indenture which sold and conveyed to Hiram A. Norris, a resident of Stockton, a parcel of land for $4000. The parcel was located in the town of Stockton. It was described as Lot No. 9 in Block 1, west of Centre Street. The property began 75 feet from the corner of the intersection of Weber's Levee and Center Street and ran 25 feet in a westerly direction along the levee; it ran 60 feet south, and thus formed a lot 25 feet by 60 feet. Charles Weber, the founder of Stockton, signed the indenture in front of witnesses Walter Herron and Edward Rhemick. This deed from Charles M. Weber to Hiram A. Norris was located in Book A, page 84 of deeds in the San Joaquin County Courthouse. The deed was filed on May 31, 1850.

The next land transaction occurred on August 20, 1850, again between Hiram A. Norris and Charles M. Weber. In this transaction Hiram A. Norris sold the same parcel back to Charles M. Weber for the consideration $4,500. Thus, Hiram Norris made a profit of $500 in less than four months time. The August 20, 1850, date may be very significant because this may be soon before he left California and returned home to his business in Brooklyn, New York. Hiram's presence in Stockton on that date is notarized by E.M. Howison. These indentures and their copies were discovered in both the Weber Collection in the Bancroft Library in Berkeley, California and in the court house in Stockton. As discussed earlier, the date of the letter of reply to the criticism of Norris, Gregg, & Norris coins appeared in the Stockton Times on Saturday morning, April 6, 1850. Is it possible that Hiram grew tired of the coin controversy after May 1, 1850, and decided to return east by late 1850?

The map below shows the location of the land, Lot 9, Block 1, both purchased and sold in 1850. It was located between Center Street and Commerce Street; the northern edge of the lot bordered on Weber's Levee. The pictures of that era would indicate that the lot was an extremely valuable piece of property as it was located next to the dock area where the sailing ships would unload. A photo of the lot in 1850 appears below [courtesy of the San Joaquin County Historical Society and Museum].

The Stockton city maps of the 1850's show the location of the lot. It was the second lot to the west of Center Street in Block 1.

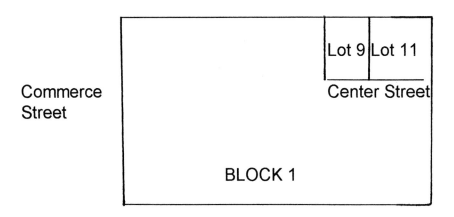

Today, in the spring of 2001, a stone monument with a brass plaque commemorates the location of Hiram Norris' lot. It reads:

HEAD OF NAVIGATION
FOR THE STOCKTON CHANNEL IN 1849 WAS
AT EL DORADO STREET. SAILING SHIPS
AND PADDLEWHEEL STEAMBOATS MADE
THE STOCKTON LEVEES A MAJOR SUPPLY
CENTER FOR THE SOUTHERN MINES DURING
THE GOLD RUSH. IN 1933, THE PORT OF STOCKTON
BECAME CALIFORNIA'S FIRST MODERN INLAND
SEAPORT.

Hiram A. Norris

Hiram A. Norris' signature was next discovered in a will that he made in Stockton, California, on November 2, 1850. Thus, he was still in California in late 1850. Hiram was married to Frances Henrietta Norris; he had previously adopted her daughter, Henrietta D. Barker. Together, Hiram A. and

Frances Henrietta had a child, Henry Selden Norris. Hiram's mother, who lived in New Haven, Connecticut was named in the will in addition to his brother, Thomas H. Norris, who was still in Brooklyn. Hiram's will was not proved until December 3, 1853 in Kings County, New York.

In mid-March, 1850, the ship the 'Georgia' left New York with 700 gold-seekers. Almost exactly a year later the 'Georgia' returned to New York with 320 passengers, along with the California mail, and their bounty of half a million dollars of gold. On the ship was a '49er with enough stories to last a lifetime. The Brooklyn Daily Eagle reported: "Return.---We were gratified a day or two since, to meet with our old friend, Hiram Norris, Esq., who returned from California in the 'Georgia', which reached New York on Saturday last. He appears to be in excellent health and spirits, and is even younger than when he left us two years ago. Mrs. Norris, who has been with her husband for the last year, came home with him; and actually gives out that she enjoyed the jaunt forth and back."[188]

By the United States census of 1860, Hiram and Frances Henrietta had had another son, Dudley Norris who was born in 1852 or 1853. By 1860 Frances Henrietta had married William T. Shannon, who had previously witnessed Hiram's will.

The 1860 census found Frances Henrietta living in New Jersey; her son Henry was age 11 and son Dudley was age 7. The two sons had both been born in New York. Frances Henrietta Shannon (previously Norris), listed the value of her real estate as $10,000 and personal assets as $30,000.

By 1870, the family had moved back to Brooklyn; Henry was not living at home any longer, but Dudley was age 17 and

---

[188]Brooklyn Daily Eagle, March 12, 1851, Page 2.

129

still living at home. Frances Henrietta did not list her assets in the 1870 census.

In the 1880 census, Henry Seldon Norris and Hiram's adopted daughter, Henrietta, were living back at home with their mother and William Shannon. By 1880, Hiram A. Norris' wife, Frances had reached the age of 58 as had her second husband, William Shannon. It is interesting that in the 1860 census William had listed his occupation as gentleman, but in the 1870 and 1880 census forms, he listed his occupation as dentist. By 1880, Henry, Hiram's son was a physician and Dudley, his other son, was a law student.

It was impossible to find Dudley's or Henry's names in the 1900 census, but in the 1910 version, Dudley was 57 years old and was employed as an engineer; Henry S. Norris, the older son was 62 years old and was still a physician.

Because the two boys were so young at the time of their father's death, in 1853, one wonders if they ever knew the story of Hiram A. Norris' adventures in the gold rush of 1849. Henry must have been born in 1852 or 1853, shortly before his father's death. Did they ever realize the mystery that their father had left behind for numismatic history to uncover?

Thomas H. Norris

Thomas H. Norris, brother of Hiram A. Norris, worked at the same company as Hiram did. During the gold rush years, 1848 to 1851, he lived at 268 Jay Street. During the 1850's he moved to Green Avenue and then to Washington Avenue. By 1880 he lived at 458 Lafayette Avenue; this was the same street upon which Hiram's widow Frances lived. She lived at 112 Lafayette Avenue.

In the 1860 census, Elizabeth Norris, the mother of Hiram and Thomas, was living in Brooklyn with Thomas; she was 85 years old. As Hiram's family had had Irish servants,

Thomas employed a German servant, Barbara Veit, who was 22.

By June 8, 1870, Thomas listed real estate assets of $150,000 and was 61 years old. Living in the same household were four members of the Powers family. The two male Powers were retired merchants, born in New York. George Powers and William Powers listed real assets of $180,000 and $70,000 respectively, and by their mid-40's both had retired. The two families living at the same house employed four domestic servants and two coachmen. In the 1870 census neither Thomas nor his wife listed any occupations.

In the 1880 census Thomas listed his occupation as retired iron manufacturer, and he was 71 years old. He was no longer married to Elizabeth, who was one year younger than himself, but was married to Emily, age 51, twenty years younger. By 1880 he had only one servant.

His will, which was written on October 18, 1895, was proved in Kings County, New York, on January 7, 1896. He too had a child, Frances Mary Norris, who was born about the time of the gold rush in 1849 or 1850. In the 1880 census, Frances ws listed as Frances M.N. Hallock; her husband was a florist. This couple had two daughters. Neither Frances, nor her husband Edward Hallock were found in later censuses. Frances made her will on May 11, 1906, on Long Island. The will was recorded on December 21, 1906, after her death.

It has been impossible to locate other descendents of Thomas Norris. Had his daughter, Frances, ever learned of the gold rush adventures of her father and her uncle, Hiram?

Charles Gregg

In numismatic history, the name and the role of Charles Gregg has been a mystery. In May of 1849, the Alta California newspaper spelled his name 'Grieg' as one of the partners producing the first territorial gold coins in California. Another expert, U.S. Assayer Augustus Humbert, spelled the name 'Grigg'. The U.S. census of 1860 spelled his name 'Greigh'. However, the Directory of New York City of 1849, as did all subsequent legal records, spelled his last name correctly as Charles Gregg.

The name Charles Gregg was in the Brooklyn directories every year from 1849 through 1871, except for 1850. It is therefore surmised that Gregg had traveled to California, probably with Hiram Norris, in 1849.

In the 1860 census, Charles was listed as 51 years old, and his occupation was merchant. He listed real property having a value of $20,000. His wife was Adeline, age 50. In the 1870 census his occupaiton was listed as 'iron pipe'; his estate was valued at $53,000. Two daughters were listed: Lucy, age 16, and Nettie, age 9, in the 1860 census. When Charles left for California his daughter must have been about age 5, and Nettie was not born until Charles returned to Brooklyn after the gold rush.

Charles Gregg's will was dated October 26, 1870, and it was proved on January 15, 1872. He had left everything to his wife. His wife Adaline's will was dated August 2, 1891, and proved on April 27, 1892. Her assets were left to two daughters and two granddaughters. The daughters were Lucy A. Dumont and Josephine A. Hillyard. The granddaughters were Elizabeth R. Hull and Florence G. Fisher.

By the time of the 1880 census, Lucy was 35 years old and married to Henry Dumont whose occupation was wholesale oil. They had one son, Charles, and two daughters. Charles was 11.

By the 1900 census, Henry Dumont was a stock broker, and son Charles was a clerk for a steamship company. This census gave the following birthdates: Henry Dumont, January 1846; Lucy Dumont, June 1845; and Charles Gregg Dumont,

September 1868. Did Charles Greg Dumont realize that he was the namesake of a gold coiner in the gold rush? Also the name of Blanche T. Dumont appears.

By the 1920 census Charles G. Dumont was 51 and did not list assets or an occupation. Charles G. Dumont and his wife Harriet had a daughter age 22 named Blanche T. Dumont. On October 16, 1920, Blanche T. Dumont married a man named Joseph F. Hunter; the marriage occurred in Rochester, New York. Blanche Hunter was born on March 2, 1897 and died on December 29, 1972.

Mrs. Blanche (Dumont) Hunter was survived by one daughter, Mrs. H. Whitney Dodge, who is still living as of the date of this publication on the east coast of the United States. She is the great, great, grandaughter of Charles Gregg, the coiner. It appears that the three coiners, or at least two of them left their business in Brooklyn and traveled to the gold rush in San Francisco. After moving to Benicia and on to Stockton, California, they returned home to Brooklyn to operate a very successful business and to raise families. How little of the history of their gold rush adventures appears to have been passed down through the generations. The last of the relatives of the coining triad is the only remaining link to the excitement of the gold rush.

Hiram Norris

Hiram Norris, who returned to Brooklyn after the gold rush, met his fate during an extreme heat wave during August, 1853. The front pages of both the New York Times and the New York Herald carried long lists of those who were victims of the heat.

The New Nork Times reported, "The effects of the present unusually hot weather are truly tragical, and resemble more the results of an epidemic, than the ordinary consequences of an increased temperature. Since Tuesday morning no less than 188 deaths have occurred, in this city alone, that have been brought under the coroner's notice, the whole of which were either from direct exposure to the sun's rays, or from over-exertion in a heated atmosphere. To prove that exposure to the sun is not necessary to produce fatal results, we may mention that yesterday afternoon, a printer in the composing room of the Herald office, while picking up types at his frame, fell suddenly dead from the effects of the heat."[189]

Editorials soon appeared in the newspapers calling for someone to help the poor laborers who were being forced to continue working in the heat. The Herald wrote, "Cannot something be done by extensive employers and contractors, in this city, to guard their workers from the peril of sun stroke? The fearful number of cases of that character which have occurred here and in the neighboring cities of Brooklyn and Williamsburg, during the last few days - particularly yesterday, when there was the number of fifty-four deaths registered with the coroner - enjoin the stern necessity of ceasing from work,

---

[189]New York Times, August 13, 1853.

in places where the laborer is exposed to the sun's rays, for at least two or three of the midday hours."[190]

Even in Brooklyn the heat was terrific. The Herald reported, "The effect of the intense hot weather of the past three days, in Brooklyn, has been truly frightful. Up to last evening, Coroner Ball held inquests upon twenty-one persons, while a number of bodies were awaiting at various places, for his offices, previous to internment."[191] "A continuous line of funerals traversed Hamilton Avenue during the whole of yesterday."[192] Hiram died during this heat wave.

Hiram Norris' obituary was lengthy in the Brooklyn paper. It reported:

> "Yesterday morning he was apparently as well as usual, and ate his dinner with the family at the usual hour without signs of disease about him. Soon after dinner he stepped out into the yard in the sun without his hat, which is supposed in some way to have excited the attack of which he died. He soon after complained of pain in the chest, which continued, with severe palpitation of the heart, for something more than an hour, when he breathed his last. Mr. Norris was a brother of Rev. W.H. Norris, a few years ago the minister of the Sands Street Methodist Church. He was educated at the West Point Military Academy, under the charge of the United States Government, and was a man of great energy of character and intellectual force. He did not, however, devote his life to military pursuits, but belonged to the firm of Norris, Gregg, & Norris, Machinists, New York, where his scientific acquirements were highly valued and brought into frequent requisition. Soon after the gold discoveries in California were made, Mr. Norris repaired to the Pacific, and was absent some two years, during which time he was profitably employed in giving the form of currency to the precious metal."[193]

---

[190]New York Herald, August 13, 1853, Page 2.
[191]New York Herald, August 14, 1853, Page 1.
[192]Brooklyn Daily Eagle, August 15, 1853, Page 2.
[193]Brooklyn Daily Eagle, August 13, 1853, Page 3.

The obituary notice said, "On Friday, Aug. 12, Hiram A. Norris, in the 48th year of his age. The relatives and friends are requested to attend his funeral, from his late residence, No. 276 Bridge St., Brooklyn, to-morrow, (Sunday), at 2 P.M., without further notice."[194] How ironic, a man who had survived the voyage to California, and had also survived the gold rush, would succumb in Brooklyn at the early age of 48. His tombstone has the age of 47 carved on it. The funeral was to be held in his home, one block from Gold Street, another irony. It is estimated that Hiram was born in the year of 1806; he died August 12, 1853. His grave is adjacent to the grave of Thomas, and is located on lot 7312.

Thomas Norris

Thomas Norris made his will in Brooklyn on October 18, 1895. For the purposes of this book, one bequest is of particular importance.

> I give and bequeath to the Greenwood Cemetery Association the sum of two thousand dollars, the interest accruing from which is to be applied to keeping in good order and repair the monuments head stones posts railings and plots of ground standing in the names of Thomas H. Norris and Hiram A. Norris adjoining each other on Locust Avenue near the shelter house in the said Greenwood Cemetery, the payment to be made to the cemetery association within two years after decease.[195]

Thomas A. Norris died on December 19, 1895, at his residence, 406 Jefferson Avenue, at the age of 88. The funeral was held Saturday evening, December 21, 1895, in his home. By the year of his death, President Cleveland had sent

---

194New York Times, August 13, 1853, Page 8.
195Will of Thomas H. Norris, Page 1.

a message to Congress asking for new policies to stop the drain of gold from the Treasury; $16,000,000 of gold had been withdrawn in one month. Mayor Schieren was advocating running the trolley line across the Brooklyn Bridge to New York City. The world had certainly changed since the gold rush of 1849. Thomas had been born on April 27, 1808, and his tomb is located in lot 7311 of the cemetery.

Charles Gregg

Charles Gregg was born on September 6, 1809, and he died on December 27, 1871. He is buried on lot 14457 in the Greenwood Cemetery. The year of his death was a year of excitement in New York. Colonel James Fisk was murdered in the Grand Central Hotel. His last visitor, as he lay dying, was Jay Gould, another famous financier. The same newspaper that reveals Gregg's death contains an article telling about the arrest of Brigham Young, at age 71, with two others for the alleged murder of Yates and Buck. It was Young that had been responsible for the coining of the Mormon gold pieces of 1848. Charles Gregg's world had changed too.

Our first major conflict of the Revolutionary War was fought at the Battle of Brooklyn on August 27, 1776. In the end, the three coiners after battling the many miles from Brooklyn to San Francisco, the primitive gold-camp conditions, and the epidemics of cholera and smallpox, reached their final resting places in the beautiful, verdant hills of Greenwood Cemetery where the Battle was fought.